The Berrigans

"They have a disturbing habit of posing hard questions, not only by what they say, but by what they do."

Noam Chomsky

"If they *free* us to make our own protests in our own ways, they also *bind* us to make those protests more sharply tomorrow than we did yesterday, and to face the uncomfortable possibility that what we may be called upon to do next week is of a magnitude we would not even have considered last month."

Robert McAfee Brown

"They have achieved at least this: they have challenged in the public mind the automatic identification of American Catholicism with the status quo."

Father Edward Duff

"Meeting Phil Berrigan was not like meeting a priest, but like meeting a military man, a general or a guerilla leader."

Wayne Hayashi,
a young war re-
sister in Hawaii

The Berrigans

Edited by
William VanEtten Casey, S. J.
and Philip Nobile

AVON
PUBLISHERS OF
DISCUS · CAMELOT · BARD

Grateful acknowledgements are made for
the following articles which appeared
for the first time in the publications
shown below:

Phil Berrigan in Prison by Philip Nobile appeared in
substantially shorter form in The New York Review of Books.
Copyright © 1970 The New York Review.
The Berrigans: Radical Activism Personified by
Gordon C. Zahn appeared in Catholic World.
Copyright © 1971 by the Missionary Society of St. Paul
the Apostle in the State of New York.
Father Dan Berrigan: Fugitive from Injustice by Paul Cowan,
and *Letter to the Weathermen* by Daniel Berrigan, S.J.
appeared in The Village Voice. Reprinted by permission of
The Village Voice. Copyrighted by the Village Voice, Inc.
© 1970, 1971.

AVON BOOKS
A division of
The Hearst Corporation
959 Eighth Avenue
New York, New York 10019

First Avon Printing, June, 1971

Printed in the U.S.A.

CONTENTS

William Van Etten Casey, S.J.

Foreword

This book is an expanded version of the special
Berrigan issue of the *Holy Cross Quarterly* of January 1971 and contains all the articles in that issue,
with one exception. The new material consists of
Gordon Zahn's article, the texts of the Harrisburg
indictment and the joint public statement of the
accused, and six articles collected by Philip Nobile:
those of Robert Coles, Rosemary Ruether, Jim Forest, Paul Cowan, the Four Families, and Dan Berrigan's Letter to the Weathermen.

The only article in the *Quarterly* that is omitted
here is one by Fr. Andrew M. Greeley who refused
permission to reprint his piece. Fr. Greeley's broad-
side made harsh accusations against the Berrigans, in strong language. Noam Chomsky's essay,
in considering some of the hard questions raised by
the Berrigans, responds to Greeley at some length.
Those references are left intact since the questions
are part of the public debate surrounding the Berrigans—though Greeley stated them in rather more
intemperate language than one is used to encounter-
ing in rational debate. Chomsky quotes or para-
phrases Greeley's charges carefully.

The Greeley view was a good sample of the

extremist rhetoric of some of the anti-Berrigan feeling and it was one of the factors that helped give birth to the special issue of the *Holy Cross Quarterly* devoted to the Berrigans. Since Dan and Phil were articulate activists and charismatic leaders who aroused conflicting emotions and generated passionate controversy, I felt that we had to begin the search for answers to the problems they posed for us. Their words and deeds disturbed, challenged and threatened us.

What changed these two young priests engaged in altruistic ministries and sent them behind bars as enemies of society? What brought them to such a pitch of heart and mind that they were willing to challenge the authority of the state? Are they prophets pointing to the disintegrating fabric of a corrupt society? victims of ruthless bureaucrats and soulless judges? martyrs in a just cause? Or are they self-righteous fanatics? arrogant nihilists? grandstanders on an ego trip?

And would a close look at their lives and personalities change us as they themselves had been changed?

When F.B.I. agents posing as birdwatchers bagged Dan Berrigan on Block Island in August 1970 and the silence of Danbury prison then enveloped both Dan and Phil, the time seemed opportune for an appraisal of them. For the next few years at least they would be dead to the world and any development they now underwent would be unknown to us on the outside. At this stage in their lives they had completed one distinct part of their work and it was now possible to assess the significance of the Berrigans with less fear of new developments requiring further changes in judgment.

The *Quarterly* seemed the natural place for such an evaluation because Holy Cross is a Jesuit college that has links with these two brothers. Dan is a Jesuit and Phil is an alumnus of the class of 1950. With the encouragement of the recently appointed President of the College, Fr. John E. Brooks, S.J., I invited a group of writers to contribute their views and to explore the meaning of the Berrigans for us and for our times.

What began as an academic exercise for the *Quarterly* took on political overtones when in late November 1970 the F.B.I. director, J. Edgar Hoover, announced to a startled nation through his willing mouthpiece, Sen. Robert C. Byrd, chairman of the Senate appropriations subcommittee, that Phil and Dan Berrigan were the leaders of a plot to blow up government heating systems and kidnap Henry Kissinger. Some reasons for Hoover's shockingly irresponsible action can be guessed with fair confidence. His professional vanity had been badly wounded in the previous spring when Dan Berrigan went underground for four months and made Keystone Kops of Hoover's agents as he led them a merry chase across the countryside. He also felt personally betrayed by these Catholic radicals because in the past he knew he could always rely on the Catholics to staff his agency and support his simplistic anti-Communism. His bitterness can be gauged by the fact that this was the first time the director had lost his cool and turned public accuser of individuals before indictments were returned.

In mid-January just as the issue was about to go to press, the Justice Department dropped the other shoe when Attorney General John Mitchell personally announced that a Federal grand jury in Harrisburg, Pa., had indicted Phil Berrigan and five others for conspiring to bomb buildings and kidnap Kissinger. ("Kidnap Kissinger?" one of the defendants later said incredulously. "That's almost as ridiculous as our other plot to spring Phil Berrigan and have him elope with Martha Mitchell.") Dan Berrigan and six others were named as co-conspirators but not indicted, a vicious legal maneuver in which the government publicly accuses a person but admits that it has no evidence to prove its accusation. I was convinced then that the Administration was bent on political persecution, not legal prosecution, of the Berrigans and their followers. This became even clearer when reporters subsequently turned up the fact that the indictment was based entirely on the testimony of a paid informer, an *agent provocateur*, who has a long history of crime and deception.

I immediately ordered a much larger than usual press run for the *Quarterly* and under the rubric, *"Who will rid me of these troublesome priests?—* Henry II to J. Edgar Hoover," I added the following coda to my editorial in that issue:

> The Administration is furious with the Berrigans. That is clear. It is also clear that someone—either the Hoover-Mitchell team or the brothers Berrigan—is lying, because the latter have categorically denied all charges. For me, the choice is easy. I stand by the Berrigans. I am convinced of their innocence. Therefore I brand Hoover and Mitchell as cowardly, contemptible and malicious in their persecution of the Berrigans.

> I welcome their retaliation. I invite their investigation.

> I have lived 57 years, 39 as a Jesuit, 27 as a priest.

After all those years of caution, a little of the Berrigan courage has finally rubbed off on me.

Thank you, Dan and Phil.

Six months later I see no reason to revise a single word in this conclusion.

Perhaps the reader of this book will also find here new courage in his own conscience and new strength in his own spirit to do whatever he can in his own life to turn our country around and return it to the ideals that inspired its foundation.

That is the message of the Berrigans.

Edward Duff, S.J.

The Burden of the Berrigans

A brother of mine has been in the United States Federal Correctional Institution at Danbury, Connecticut, since last August; and in addition, the government has now named him, but not indicted him, as a co-conspirator in a plot to kidnap Henry Kissinger and to blow up heating tunnels in Washington.

I have never met Daniel Berrigan, nor, given our differences of temperament and experience, is it sure that we would like one another. Yet Dan Berrigan is a personal problem. Not an embarrassment, mind you: he has been publicly certified as being in good standing as a priest and as a Jesuit by his Provincial Superior and undoubtedly enjoys the affectionate and enthusiastic endorsement of the younger members of the Society. It is not, then, his being in jail—along with his blood brother, Josephite Father Philip Berrigan—that is disconcerting. It is Dan Berrigan's spiritual stance and political posture that challenge me as a priest and as a political scientist. For my own clarity of mind, I must come to terms with the issues the Berrigans personify and publicize. They are a burden.

The burden would not be lightened by a visit to my brother Jesuit at Danbury, although I am old enough to recognize the project as listed among the Corporal Works of Mercy. I prefer not to risk the experience of Ralph Waldo Emerson calling at the Concord jail to see his friend, Henry Thoreau, sentenced for refusing to pay taxes to a town that supported drilling for the Mexican War, a war which he deemed a move to extend slavery.

The exponent of Self-Reliance was puzzled by the situation: "Henry," he asked, "why are you here?"

"Waldo, why are you *not* here?" was the curt reply.

Factually, Daniel Berrigan is in prison because on May 17, 1968, with eight others, including his priest-brother, he invaded the offices of Local Board 33 on the second floor of the Knights of Columbus Hall in the Baltimore suburb of Catonsville. In a well-planned operation, three hundred files were hurriedly rifled, quickly dumped into wire trash-baskets and burned with home-made napalm in the parking lot amid prayers and the whir of television cameras. As to why he destroyed government property and interfered with the workings of the Selective Service System, the two counts on which the jury convicted him after a perfunctory, half-hour consideration, Daniel Berrigan has been prolix and eloquent both at the trial and in many subsequent interviews. These explanations were frequent during the nearly four months he evaded the F.B.I. when ordered to prison on April 9 following the rejection by the Supreme Court of his appeal last March. After having been sheltered by thirty-seven different families in twelve cities, Daniel Berrigan was captured on August 11 at the summer home on Block Island, R.I., of William Stringfellow, Episcopal lay theologian and lawyer whose years defending Harlem's poor are recounted in *My People Is the Enemy*. The book includes the caustic (and challenging) comment: "Christianity is about religion, not about life."

One of Berrigan's courtroom explanations of his multiple motivation for the burning of the draft records involved an excursus on St. Ignatius' program of operation: "we [Jesuits] belonged actually in society, in the culture, in the schools, in the ghettos among the poor, as the servants of men, and that it was there that we would find God or nowhere." Asked by defense counsel whether the Catonsville demonstration was "carrying out that philosophy of the Jesuit Order," Daniel Berrigan affirmed: "May I say that if that is not accepted as a substantial part of my action, then the action is eviscerated of all meaning and I should be committed for insanity."

Daniel Berrigan is a poet and, as national awards attest, a very good poet. He is, then, a person of imaginative insight, a master of metaphor, a stylist of shining affirmation but, most significant, he is an artist of acute and resonant sensibility.

A couple of months before his trial Father Berrigan had flown to Hanoi to accept three American P.O.W.s the North Vietnamese regime had chosen to release. While he was in the city, a U.S. bombing raid forced all to flee to improvised shelters. The priest climbed down into the hole, an infant in his arms being fed all the while by its sister. In a poem he began composing, the American Jesuit saw all the purpose of a better world and all the evil of our foreign policy caught up in the fate of that Oriental baby.

Nor should one think that Berrigan arrived in Vietnam as an innocent abroad. He had examined at first hand the moral monstrosity of *apartheid* in South Africa and had talked with the survivors of the Sharpeville massacre; during an enforced "vacation" he had inspected the teeming *favellas,* the fetid off-scourings of the bourgeoning cities of Latin America; he had experienced the efforts of Catholicism to endure and adapt under oppression in East Europe. And now he sees American civilization as ugly, menacing and irremediably corrupt. He anticipates, moreover, that all thoughtful men will come to "the dawning realization that practically nothing of traditional civilized structures is functioning for human welfare. This is true of medicine, education, communication, arts, the Church, and indeed, God help us, the courts." Daniel Berrigan believes that the American political order has lost its moral legitimacy.

Since I do not share such an apocalyptic judgment, I must ask if an insensitiveness to evil is responsible.

When Catherine Genovese returned late at night from her lunchroom cashier's job to her apartment house on Austin Street in the New York suburb of Kew Gardens on March 13, 1964, she was attacked by a man who assaulted her on the street as she sought safety and finally stabbed her to death in an entryway. For more than an hour 38 neighbors watched the crime being committed without coming to her aid or calling the police. It is easy to forget Erich Fromm's observation that the opposite of love is not hate but apathy.

Was I guilty of this apathy when just before Christmas, 1961, I passed without second thought American G.I.s lined up at the Thansanhut airport, Saigon? In the city I stayed at the Metropole, an old French era hotel with ice-cream-parlor-style fans in the ceiling, across the square from the new air-conditioned Caravelle, where the International Control Commission and the U.S. brass relaxed. Accepted as *un Canadien de la langue anglaise* by the staff (an error to be encouraged in all countries), I was persuaded that all the people I met were already weary of war. But President John F. Kennedy, I recalled, had declared in his inaugural address: "Let every nation know, whether it wishes us well or ill, that we shall pay any price, bear any burden, meet any hardship, support any friend, oppose any foe, in order to assure the survival and the success of liberty." A few days before my arrival in Saigon, Kennedy had written to President Diem that "we shall promptly increase our assistance to your defense. . . ." G.I.s at the airport in 1961, then, seemed normal.

Nor, on reflection, was I disturbed for long— is "radicalized" the word?—by the *bustis* in Calcutta, those rabbit warrens for the wretched people fortunate to have some kind of a roof over their heads. An extraordinary Albanian nun, Mother Theresa, took me to her House for the Dying, two garage-like sheds beside a noisy pagan temple, where derelicts from the streets are brought and nursed, the unlucky ones recovering enough to return to the streets—to starve again. A ten-dollar handshake and the promise of publicity for her manifold charities unburdened me emotionally of Mother Theresa and the limitless human misery in Calcutta. Was I the Levite who hurried along

the road to Jericho (presumably on Jesuit business), untouched by the plight of those whose
humanity had been plundered? But plundered by
whom? And what were the possibilities of effective
action open to me?

Last May 23, in the course of a public conference
at Orleans in France Dom Helder Camara, Archbishop of Recife, Brazil, termed "scandalous" the
sale by the Pompidou government of sixteen Mirage
III fighter-bombers to his country, especially in
view of the desperate needs of the poor. Given the
documented evidence of tortures by the military
regime in Brazil, Catholic and Protestant groups
demanded the cancellation of the arms sale, with
two Catholics, a priest and a lay professor, under-
taking a two-week, public fast in protest. Their
action was endorsed by the bishop of Orleans,
Guy-Marie Riobé, who declared: "It would not
be honest to applaud Dom Helder and then let
him alone bear the considerable risk of this matter
without ourselves sharing on the spot the same
struggle." The U.S. government will sell, finance
and give away more than $6.7 billion in arms
in 1971 to other governments, many of dubious
origin and disputable legitimacy. Ostensibly to
strengthen the collective defense of the West, such
arms have been used in wars by opposing nations
—Pakistan and India, Israel and Jordan. Deplore
the practice though I do, I see no feasible, effective
protest to stop the program. Is this acquiescence
in evil or spiritual sloth or passive cooperation?

On the other hand, as a teacher I am (presumably) preparing collegians for what Vatican II
calls "the layman's own distinctive role." Perhaps
through cowardice I have interpreted the text that
follows that phrase as a counsel of caution:

Often enough the Christian view of things will itself suggest some specific solution in certain circumstances. Yet it happens rather frequently, and legitimately so, that with equal sincerity some of the faithful will disagree with others on a given matter. Even against the intentions of their proponents, however, solutions proposed on one side or another may be easily confused by many people with the gospel message. Hence it is necessary for people to remember that no one is allowed in the aforementioned situations to appropriate the Church's authority for his opinion. They should always try to enlighten one another through honest discussion, preserving mutual charity and caring above all for the common good.

Serving the common good in my present enterprise is sensitizing young minds to injustice and official hypocrisy, cauterizing the instinctive but idolatrous admiration of American power and affluence, and unfolding the implications of the verdict of Pope Paul VI in his encyclical *On the Development of Peoples:* "The world is sick. Its illness consists less in the unproductive monopolization of resources by a small number of men than in a lack of brotherhood among individuals and peoples."

Father Berrigan's political pessimism is total. "American power," he tells us, "is locked into its method, its sleep-walking, its nightmare, its rampant and irreversible character. No change in the personnel of power seems to bring about any serious change in the functioning and direction of power, in the misuse and grinding under of human beings." A case can be argued for such a bleak judgment, but one wonders how the Berrigan brief for such a conclusion would read beyond an enunciation of the failure to convince a judge and jury that a clear intent to stop the war in Vietnam merited an acquittal.

From his brother, Philip, Dan Berrigan learned of the plight of black people in New Orleans and Baltimore; from several of his Catonsville co-defendants he heard brutal details of U.S. government support of oppressive, reactionary regimes in Latin America. But from his collegians at Cornell and from the professional people—the professors and doctors and clergymen—who harbored him in the underground he scarcely encountered evidence of American power in the "grinding under of human beings." When captured on Block Island, he was reading "The Trial and Death of Socrates." Earlier he had told an interviewer: ". . . in the way of contemporary poetry I am particularly enjoying Allen Ginsberg and Denise Levertov."

This is all proper fare for a poet and poets are in short supply these days. It seems, however, inadequate resource material for dire political assessments which invite (and expect) an analysis of how we got where we are and some suggestions as to what directions we should move. The situation is too serious for stridency or hand-wringing.

We got where we are because of a decision, made early in the Kennedy Administration and supported routinely by our freely elected representatives that—in addition to maintaining our nuclear superiority—this nation must be prepared to fight simultaneously two-and-a-half conventional wars, a major war in Europe, another in Asia and a brush-fire operation in Latin America. The result has been a blind distortion of national priorities with social decay at home accepted as the price of power abroad, with fifty cents of the tax dollar going for military or para-military expenditures and one in every ten jobs dependent directly or indirectly on our military posture. This development has been fostered by intelligent men of good will; it has been rubber-stamped regularly by Congress; it has been supported by the trade unions and industry and accepted by the American citizenry. The issue, then, is immensely larger than the Vietnam war.

In fact, it is only now that we can see that our pursuit of world security has made it unsafe to walk the streets of our own cities, including the nation's capital, at night. We are pledged to defend forty-two countries (our troops are stationed in no less than thirty) and yet we face disintegration at home. The gravity of our situation was expressed in an editorial in last June's *Fortune*, the monthly edited, it claims, for "the men in charge of change":

> For the first time, it is no longer possible to take for granted that the U.S. will somehow survive the crisis that grips it. The land will survive, of course, along with the machines and the people—or most of them. But no nation is merely, or mainly, an aggregate of its geography, its material assets and its warm bodies. At the core of the U.S., conferring identity, cohesion, belief and vitality, stands a Proposition: free men, despite differences of status, belief and interest, can govern themselves. Upon the survival of that Proposition, confirmed by eight generations of superb achievement, depends any worthwhile future that an entity called the United States might have. And it is that Proposition—amazingly— which in the spring of 1970 has come to be at stake.

Clouding the future of that Proposition has been a distortion of national goals in the exaltation of exorbitant military powers, a process briefed in such current books as Richard J. Barnet's *The Economy of Death*, Seymour Melman's *Pentagon Capitalism*, Senator William Proxmire's *Report from Wasteland*, Sidney Lens' *The Military-Industrial Complex*, Colonel James A. Donovan's *Militarism U.S.A.*, J. K. Galbraith's *How to Control the Military*, Senator Fulbright's *The Pentagon Propaganda Machine*, Bruce M. Russett's *What Price Vigilance?*, Richard F. Kaufman's *The War Profiteers*, Adam Yarmolinsky's *The Military Establishment: Its Impact on American Society*, and George Thayer's *The War Business*.

Such literature strikes me as more apposite to the serious protestors of the Vietnam war than the collected works of Mohandas Gandhi in the Berrigan library. For what, after all, is the American equivalent of a march to the sea to make your own salt or weaving your own cloth for your own *dhoti* on your own spinning wheel, when the news of the preliminary award of the B-1 bomber (a program estimated to cost eventually $12 billion) to North American Rockwell Corporation is headlined by the Los Angeles *Times* as "43,000 NEW JOBS!" Or when the only dispute in the Senate last September over $2.5 billion for thirty new destroyers was whether half should be built at the Bath Iron Works in Senator Margaret Chase Smith's state of Maine or all of them at the Litton shipyards at Pascagoula in Armed Services Committee Chairman John Stennis' fief of Mississippi?

Ours is undoubtedly a society fearsomely preoccupied by war and mired in the making of ever more lethal and costly weapons—and this to the

crying neglect of urgent national problems. To
say, however, that it has shut its ears to public
challenge, that it is controlled by those "grinding
under human beings" is certainly questionable,
not least in view of the audience commanded by
Father Berrigan during his months of evading
arrest when his articles and interviews appeared
in the *Saturday Review, Commonweal, New Yorker,
New York Review of Books, Christian Century,
New York Times Magazine* and *Village Voice,* along
with network appearances on the National Broad-
casting Company and the National Educational
Television, plus a play of his, "The Trial of the
Catonsville Nine," produced in Los Angeles.

Believing that "the times are inexpressibly evil,"
Daniel Berrigan believes also that they are irretriev-
ably beyond lawful remedy. He asserts: "Let me
say as plainly as I know how, I don't see as a
political tactic that anything that might be called
'useful' is left to us, except civil disobedience. I
say that openly. I am not supposed to say it—by
the terms of my bond—but I say it anyway. I
don't see anything remaining to us by way of
confronting the warmakers, except civil disobedience."

Here is the American tradition of Henry David
Thoreau—updated. A poet, too, who claimed to
hear "a different drummer," Thoreau insisted that
"any man more right than his neighbor constitutes
a majority of one," counseled using one's life as
"a counter friction to stop the machine," extolled
John Brown, the insurrectionist, as "an angel of
light" and advocated "direct action" in the form
of withdrawing one's allegiance to a government
permitting slavery.

While Thoreau as early as 1849 thought that "it

is not too soon for honest men to rebel and revolutionize" because of the legal protection of slavery, his knowledge of (and interest in) the complex issues involved in the Civil War was slight; his "rebellion" was a token one.

What Daniel Berrigan envisages beyond generalized civil disobedience, encouraging "a solid wall of conscience to confront the warmakers," urging people to "say NO! courageously, constantly, clearsightedly," he has not told us. He underlines the spiritual problem at issue: "Man is unready for a human future. He has not grown those organs and resources which allow him to function in an alternate way, where he lives, and to reach out with public consequences." He speaks of a new form of human community, one no longer dominated and restricted by the limitations of the "nuclear family"; he hoped that he could build bridges to the Weathermen and the Black Panthers; certainly as a priest he was pleased by his appeal to the New Left.

At their trial the Catonsville Nine argued their "noncriminal intent" in destroying the draft files, a plea that was disallowed. The facts were not in dispute: the Nine had alerted reporters and had prepared a press release in advance to assure maximum publicity and had waited patiently the arrival of the police to arrest them. Their purpose, obviously, was larger than to discommode temporarily an individual Selective Service Board. They surely must have realized that the inexorable workings of the draft system would automatically fill the gaps caused by the missing Catonsville records by increasing the calls on neighboring boards. (Did they advert to the possibility that they might be destroying the painfully compiled dossiers of some applying for Conscientious Objector status?) What they ambitioned was to subject a phase of national policy, the war, to judicial review.

They had tried all other means. Philip Berrigan had prayed in front of the homes of the Joint Chiefs of Staff at Fort Myers, Virginia, and of Secretary McNamara in Washington; he had talked with Secretary Rusk; he had interviewed senators; he had given talks against the war across the country; and, six months earlier, he had poured blood on the draft files in the United States Custom House in Baltimore. Daniel Berrigan from late 1965 had been co-chairman of "Clergy and Laymen Concerned About Vietnam"; he had been jailed in the aftermath of the march on the Pentagon at the time Philip as one of the Baltimore Four was defacing draft records with blood. Previous protests having failed, the Catonsville Nine would have the courts, the guardians of the American Proposition and the symbol of the country's civic righteousness, condemn the Executive branch of the government. By acquitting them the judiciary would, in effect, rule the Vietnam war illegal.

It was an empty effort. The prosecuting attorney conceded that in fact "reasonable men" could hold that the war is illegal, in violation of the U.S. Constitution, the United Nations Charter and the 1954 Geneva Accords. In charging the jury Judge Roszel Thomsen declared: "The law does not recognize political, religious, moral convictions, or some higher law, as justification for the commission of a crime, no matter how good the motive may be." In effect, the Judicial Branch of the government told the defendants to take their case to the public in the hope of influencing the Legislative Branch (i.e., an already too compliant Congress) in order to restrain the Executive Branch, but do this after a jail sentence for destroying government property and interfering with the draft that is keeping the war going. For, with the representatives of the people in Congress routinely voting massive appropriations for the war, it is excessive to pretend that Vietnam is merely an aberration of the Executive.

What did the action of the Berrigans at Catonsville achieve? The question, though unfair, is unavoidable. It is unfair because the defendants made it clear that they felt morally compelled to make their protest in the form that they did and were aware of the legal penalties. But was, as some allege, the tactic of burning draft records counterproductive? Last May some seven hundred campuses went on strike to protest the Cambodian extension of the Vietnam war. Subsequently, a Gallup poll revealed that 82 percent of the American people disapproved of such form of protest.

During his underground days Father Daniel Berrigan surfaced briefly as a guest preacher at the First United Methodist Church of Germantown, a Philadelphia suburb. His Sunday sermon was filmed for television, as were the reactions of some of his listeners. Three of the four people interviewed had never heard of him, despite the pastor's explicit introduction, and assumed that he was "a refractory cleric," "a defrocked priest or one of those who has left the Church." All three were elderly folk, plainly W.A.S.P.s. (The fourth, a younger man, recognized the preacher, but said that, after considerable thought, his conscience dictated a different course.)

But the Berrigans have achieved at least this: they have challenged in the public mind the automatic identification of American Catholicism with the status quo, its alliance with prevailing patriotic causes, its ambition to be accepted, not so much as an alien value-system adjusting to a politically neutral environment, but as a group of citizens "just like everyone else." The example of the Berrigans raises the doubt that American Catholicism can be counted on to supply acolytes for *all* the shrines of the civic religion that is the American Way of Life. In the past Catholic sympathies and votes were deliverable on behalf of organized labor because its members were "our kind." (Or, as I once heard Reinhold Niebuhr explain, because the mill owners were Protestant.) Endeavoring to elude the hostility reserved for the poor and the late arrivals in God's Own Country, to escape the heritage of hyphenation (Irish-American! German-American! Polish-American!), we American Catholics became, all too successfully, Super-Americans, prompt to match the number of our Gold Star Mothers or our nominees for the All Star football lineup with any group in the country. One of "our kind" who made it, Daniel P. Moynihan, supplied the measure of our success: it is the Harvard men, he remarked, who are to be checked for security clearance and it is the Fordham graduates who do the checking. The ultimate scandal for the Jesuit-graduate F.B.I. agent who arrested Father Berrigan was not the complaisance of Mr. Hoover's men at violations of federal anti-discrimination laws by Southern police but the fact of a priest defying the government.

The Berrigan phenomenon notifies the nation that it is idle to look primarily to the hierarchy—

or its secretariat in Washington—to know what
American Catholics think on issues of civic controversy. Whatever was true in the days of child labor
legislation, the vote for women, national health insurance, now no longer obtains.

That Daniel Berrigan's example and charismatic
personality have strongly stimulated among younger Jesuits the conviction that Christianity has a
social message and that they are involved in its
meaning for the world seems certain. As one who
edited *Social Order*, a monthly review with precisely
that scope and function, and which died for lack
of Jesuit support, I note the change with satisfaction.

To be sure, I am often disconcerted by some
manifestations of that enthusiasm: the ease with
which gospel truths are translated into concrete
political programs, the astonishment that the problem of evil is intractable to foot-stomping, the
substitution of conscience for thought, the erection
of impatience into an ideology, the solipsism of
solution by incantation. Father Berrigan is not
wholly innocent of such tendencies himself, as
when he wishes the Society of Jesus to be "a
brotherhood which will be skilled in a simple, all
but lost art—the reading of the gospel and life
according to its faith." Would that reordering
society and righting a wounded world were as simple
as Prince Kropotkin taught and the Moral Re-
Armamenters believe.

In a letter, widely reprinted, addressed "Dear
Father General, Father Provincial and Brothers in
Christ," Daniel Berrigan explained anew his purposes, announced his continuing resistance to "the
instruments of the war makers" and sent "a word
of love to the brethren who have been for these

30 years my blood line, my family, my embodied tradition and conscience." It is an eloquent appeal for moral change, for a birth in the spirit requiring "a new aceptance of the world with all that implied: moral crisis, infamy, risk, obloquy, mistakes, *horror vacui*, misunderstanding, the ability to deal with personal and social violence, the breakup of cherished hope, the tearing apart of even the most admirable cultural fabric, the loss of all things, in fact, 'if only Christ be gained'."

Daniel Berrigan's loyalty to the ideals of the Society, then, is deep and fixed. He is undisturbed about those who leave, identifying himself with the core of *la Compagnie*, the "community in which men may speak the truth to men, in which our lives will be purified of the inhuman drives of egoism, acculturation, professional pride and dread of life." Moreover, he knows the incessant demands of permanent availability in such a career of service. "Being a celibate in this situation," he told an interviewer, "is very important. American society has sexualized itself as a ticket of admission." May it be noted, too, that when in late 1965 Father Berrigan was summarily banished from New York for his antiwar efforts by his Jesuit Superiors, yielding to ecclesiastical pressure, he went quietly, throwing no tantrums, calling no press conferences.

And so Daniel Berrigan's "cry for justice and peace" is muted behind the walls of the federal medium security prison at Danbury where he is kept busy, probably making mattress covers, certainly praying for the world. He faces the tedium of enforced idleness, the frustration of seclusion and the satisfaction of a slowly growing general revulsion over the murderous misadventure in Vietnam. To the extent that his efforts sharpened the public conscience on the futility of uncontrolled violence, his burden is lightened. He must find solace in the words Chesterton put into the mouth of Our Lady, speaking to King Alfred before the battle of Athelney, words which the London *Times* printed as its total editorial comment the morning after Dunkerque:

"I tell you naught for your comfort
    Yea, naught for your desire,
Save that the sky grows darker yet
    And the sea rises higher.
Night shall be thrice night over you
    And heaven an iron cope;
Do you have joy without a cause
    Yea faith without hope!"

The burden on this particular Jesuit, on the other hand, is clearly specified by Daniel Berrigan in his letter to his fellow members of the Society of Jesus: "I ask your prayers that my brother and I and all who are at the edge may be found faithful and obedient, in good humor, and always at your side."

This is the burden a brother Jesuit gladly bears.

Richard J. Clifford, S.J.

The Berrigans: Prophetic?

If we look to the Bible and to the history of the Christian Church, the problem of the Fathers Berrigan is not whether they are prophets, but rather whether they are true prophets. And answering that crucial question—who is a true prophet? —has been a problem from the earliest days of God's people.

The Book of Deuteronomy, a collection of homilies and laws from the eighth and seventh centuries B.C., gives some advice to those trying to discern true and false prophets. "And if you say in your heart, 'How may we know the word which the Lord has not spoken?'—when a prophet speaks in the name of the Lord, if the word does not come to pass or come true, that is a word which the Lord has not spoken; the prophet has spoken it presumptuously, you need not be afraid of him." (Deut. 18:21–22.) Whether the prophet is true or not depends on whether his word comes true, whether it is valid.

The criterion of success alone could be abused, however, and so another test was suggested. Did the prophet's teaching agree with the faith of the fathers, with the main tenets of Yahwistic belief,

or did it lead the people to abandon the one God
for the seductive gods of their pagan neighbors?
"If a prophet arises among you . . . and gives you
a sign or wonder, and the sign or wonder which
he gives you comes to pass, and if he says, 'Let us
go after other gods,' which you have not known,
'and let us serve them,' you shall not listen to the
words of that prophet." (Deut. 13-1–3.)

It was not easy, then, for the people of Israel to
decide if a prophet was "true," that is, whether he
spoke God's word. People had to look closely at
the words and actions of the man claiming to be
God's spokesman and decide for themselves whether the prophet's word proved to be true and
whether it was in accord with the authentic traditions of the fathers.

PROPHETIC UNPOPULARITY

Today we are inclined to think of the great
prophets of Israel—Amos, Isaiah, Jeremiah, and
Ezekiel—as recognized authorities in their lifetime.
This is not so. Because their main message was
unpopular—the people were to be punished with
loss of their land because of their sins—they
were opposed by powerful interests. Amos was
ordered off government property (a state-supported
shrine) for subversive preaching. Isaiah, the most
highly placed of all the prophets, consistently
opposed the royal cabinet on foreign policy.
Jeremiah's foes always outnumbered his friends
and he served time in prison for undermining
morale in time of war. The preaching of these
prophets often went counter to popular thinking
and government announcements. Their message of

judgment against Israel in all probability never would have passed into Scripture had not Jerusalem been destroyed and the people exiled, thus proving true their word of judgment.

In the New Testament, Jesus came as the True Prophet. He spoke for God as no man did. Yet when he spoke, most of his hearers did not believe and he had to die for their unbelief.

When the biblical prophet speaks, it is not to convince people of the correctness of his position with overpowering arguments. He is a spokesman for God, and God's message can only be received in faith. The prophet therefore does not compel. He invites each person to see himself, his world, and his God in a fresh way. Not every aspect of the prophet's person or message need attract his hearers nor even necessarily be factually accurate in every detail. He is not scoring debater's points. He is proclaiming God's word.

The prophet as roughhewn spokesman for God, sometimes so enwrapped in his central announcement that he is unbalanced and even incorrect in his lesser judgments, is well illustrated by some prophetic persons in the history of the Christian Church. As the Christian Church grew over the centuries, certain individuals (many not of the clergy) were able to give decisive leadership in crucial situations and to point the Church in new directions.

But the prophetic person is an individual member of the Church and his own gift of prophecy is only a limited portion of the gifts which the one Spirit gives to the Church. The prophetic individual must be in dialogue with the whole Church, particularly with the college of office holders, and must remain humbly aware that his own gift must be supplemented and augmented by the gifts of others in the Church. Even authentic prophets exercise their ministry in dialogue with the whole Church. The ministry of prophesying is frequently "messy," that is, their dialogue is not a quiet conversation with bishops and learned theologians, but a shouting match between Church members. In the course of the exchange, the truth comes out, and all the members of the Church, whether they act on the prophet's words or not, know that a prophet has been among them.

PROPHETIC "MESSINESS"

Just how "messy" prophets and their messages have been in the Christian centuries is well illustrated by prophets whom the Church has recognized as authentic, but whose own teaching contained errors. The "visions" of St. Hildegard of Bingen, of St. Elizabeth of Schonau, of St. Bridget of Sweden and St. Frances of Rome contain strange errors which these saints thought were revealed and then tried to impose on their contemporaries, including bishops, in very authoritative terms. St. Bernard of Clairvaux prophesied the success of the Second Crusade, yet lived to see it fail. St. Francis of Assisi imposed a strict command that no explanations and no papal declarations were to be added to his rule, provoking a serious crisis in his young order. St. Anthony saved the day by going against his father and appealing to the Pope. St. Vincent Ferrer proclaimed the imminent end of the world, appealing to a revelation and the miracles worked by him. St. Catherine Laboure, the visionary who propagated the Miraculous

Medal, also reported revelations which she later had to admit were erroneous.

PROPHETIC PERSONS TODAY

We have glanced at some prophets of the past to see if the Berrigan brothers have their gift. In deciding whether the Berrigans are truly prophetic, the sensitive Christian need not expect to agree with them in every point. A prophet, after all, is not the whole Church. His message may come out only after dialogue, often painful and even violent, with the whole Church. One therefore ought not to make a quick judgment: "I agree," or "I disagree." The acceptance, or nonacceptance, of a prophet is not an instant process. It takes time and other voices than the prophet's must be heard.

Nor is agreement or disagreement with his message all that a prophet should ask of us. We are to face the same issues he faces, and question ourselves seriously about them. For example, the Fathers Berrigan have forced us to see the war in Vietnam not merely as a foreign-policy problem, but as an ethical dilemma that involves each man's conscience. As obvious as the previous sentence sounds, how often do we hear and read that each citizen has a moral responsibility in his country's policies?

The Berrigans' gesture of pouring napalm on draft files and burning them, precisely because it is a symbolic gesture, fits not only the tradition of radical American politics, but also the prophetic tradition of symbolic acts. We need only recall Isaiah walking "naked and barefoot" through the streets of Jerusalem and Jeremiah burying his loincloth at the river bank. Whether we approve or not, the gesture itself concretizes vividly the moral issue of the war for many. It forces us to declare ourselves on the Vietnam war and on war in general. It disturbs the Christian community (and those outside the Christian community) and forces re-examination of old beliefs. Out of the turmoil, perhaps, a new consensus on peace and war will arise.

The Berrigans have chosen the right issue, war and more particularly the Vietnam war, which many before them had regarded as morally neutral. Their gestures and words have made it come alive. Out of the dialogue, out of the noisy and heated debate, there is likely to emerge among Christians a view of war that is different from that of the past. The Berrigans need not be correct in every detail of their analysis in order to be acknowledged as true prophets. Their message will be supplemented and ultimately judged by the whole Church. But until that day when we shall know for sure, the wise Christian ought to consider well the issues Fathers Dan and Phil Berrigan have raised.

Noam Chomsky

On the
Limits
of Civil
Disobedience

The Berrigans have a disturbing habit of posing
hard questions, not only by what they write and
say, but by what they do. A reasonable person will
admit that there exist, in principle, circumstances
under which civil disobedience, even sabotage, is
legitimate. The Berrigans have argued, with care
and patience, that such circumstances now exist:
specifically, that nonviolent resistance to the Indochina war is a legitimate response to criminal acts
of the American executive, and that a legitimate
component of such nonviolent resistance is the destruction of property that has no right to exist in
that its immediate function is to implement these
criminal acts. They have suggested that such a response is not only legitimate in principle, but also
that it may be efficacious in restricting, perhaps ter-
minating the criminal violence of the American
war. They have not been content merely to present
the argument, or—as many others have—to con-
struct the case from which the conclusion follows,
without explicitly drawing it. Rather, they have
pursued the logic of the argument to its conclusion
and have acted accordingly, destroying property
that (they argue) has no right to exist. They have

also denied that the state has the right to prosecute those who act to restrain its criminal violence; and, again, they have acted accordingly, refusing to yield themselves voluntarily to state authorities.

Such actions challenge beliefs, attitudes and assumptions that are rarely questioned, because, for one reason, questioning them is quite uncomfortable. It is, therefore, not surprising that the unconventional thinking and actions of the Berrigans sometimes call forth irrational reactions. Consider, for example, Andrew Greeley's curious discussion. He claims that Dan Berrigan is a totalitarian who would imprison those who do not accept his moral judgments, and charges him with advocating the destruction of American society, with preaching hatred for this society and its people. Such charges will astonish anyone who actually knows Dan Berrigan, or who has any familiarity with his writings. Greeley's discussion, though in fact frivolous and irresponsible, should not merely be dismissed on these grounds, with no further comment. Rather, it should be interpreted, I believe, as a testimony to the seriousness of the questions that the Berrigans pose. It is precisely because these are hard and serious questions that those who fear to face them are driven to outlandish distortion and fantastic accusations.

A serious reaction to the Berrigans' reasoning and actions will take account of the nature of the war in Southeast Asia, the functioning of American democracy, and the responsibilities of the citizen under such circumstances. One might, for example, reject their reasoning on the grounds that American intervention in Southeast Asia is legitimate (though perhaps no longer worth its cost, thus a mistake)—the dominant opinion in the United States today, I would guess; or that the intervention, though illegitimate, should not be opposed by civil disobedience, which is improper in a democracy; or that civil disobedience, though legitimate under the present circumstances, is still improper because it is ineffective (or even "counterproductive"), or because of its likely social consequences; or that civil disobedience, though legitimate and proper, should not include destruction of property and should be followed by willing submission to state authorities. These questions, and others like them, are the ones that should be raised concerning the Berrigans' choice of action—that is, their decision to act, and their choice of means. I would like to comment briefly on these matters.

THE ILLEGITIMATE WAR

Because it is, I presume, the dominant opinion in the U.S., the assumption that American intervention is legitimate (though perhaps unwise) can obviously not be ignored. I will be brief, since my own views have been presented at length elsewhere. The question of the legitimacy of the American intervention is in part a question of principle, and in part turns on the character of the American war. As to the question of principle, it seems to me quite clear that we have neither the authority nor the competence to intervene with military force in the internal affairs of Indochina. In fact, this principle is even written into law. The "supreme law of the land" (as expressed, in this case, by the United Nations Charter, a valid treaty) is quite unequivocal in this respect. It states that forceful intervention is legitimate only if authorized by the Security Council or in "collective self-defense" against armed attack.

Efforts to argue that the American intervention is not, technically, criminal, therefore seek to establish that we are engaged in collective self-defense of South Vietnam against an armed attack from the North. However, as the record clearly shows, the American intervention long preceded any direct North Vietnamese involvement, and has always been far greater in scale, a fact conceded even by the Pentagon. Senator Mansfield, who is quite well-informed about Asian affairs, stated: "When the sharp increase in the American military effort began in early 1965, it was estimated that only about 400 North Vietnamese soldiers were among the enemy forces in the South, which totalled 140,000 at that time." The Pentagon confirmed the accuracy of this statement, and, in fact, other Pentagon documents indicate that these 400 North Vietnamese soldiers were detected in late April, 1965, two and a half months after the intensive bombardment of North *and South* Vietnam was underway, at a time when the American troop level was approaching 30,000.

I will not trace the history of this sorry affair any further. There is a great deal of unchallenged documentary evidence that demonstrates, conclusively I believe, that the U.S. is not engaged in collective self-defense against an armed attack but rather, that it extended its long-term forceful intervention in Vietnam to a full-scale invasion of South Vietnam in early 1965, because the N.L.F. had won the internal civil struggle, despite the extensive (and illegal) direct American intervention.

Defenders of American actions frequently argue that questions of law are too complex for the layman and should be left to experts. However, in this case, a careful reading of the arguments, pro and con, reveals little divergence over questions of law. The issues debated are factual and historical: specifically, is the U.S. engaged in collective self-defense against armed attack from North Vietnam? This is an issue concerning which the layman is in a position to make a judgment, and the responsible citizen will not be frightened away from doing so by the claim that the matter is too esoteric for him to comprehend. Extensive documentation is available, and, I believe, it shows clearly that the American war is criminal, even in the narrowest technical sense.

THE SAVAGE WAR

When we turn to the character of the war, the issue of legalism fades. Three years and three million tons of bombs ago, Bernard Fall—no alarmist, highly knowledgeable, and fundamentally in support of American aims in Indochina though appalled by the savagery with which they were pursued—warned that "Viet-Nam as a cultural and historic entity . . . is threatened with extinction . . . [as] . . . the countryside literally dies under the blows of the largest military machine ever unleashed on an area of this size." Townsend Hoopes, undersecretary of the Air Force in the Johnson administration, writes that "the rebels of Indochina are inviting the West, which possesses unanswerable military power, to pursue its strategic logic to the final conclusion, which is genocide." A correspondent for the authoritative *Far Eastern Economic Review* compares the American war in Vietnam to "the vicious way the Germans fought across the Soviet Union," and the extremely well-informed correspondent of *Le Monde*, J. C. Pomonti, explains further that the Americans "concluded that there might be some advantage to be drawn, either in Laos or Vietnam, from the exodus caused by their bombings of the countryside and occupations of the towns. They reasoned . . . that their savage action and its results would allow them to break down the traditional socio-economic structures of the two countries, and . . . that they could thus put down a rebellion closely interwoven with these structures." The evidence in support of these characterizations of the American war is, to our endless shame, overwhelming.

For such reasons as these, I believe we must conclude that the American war in Indochina is criminal, in both the technical legal and general moral sense. The belief that the war is legitimate, though perhaps unwise, is, in my opinion, scandalous by strictly intellectual as well as decent moral standards. And it is deeply disturbing that this view is dominant. From this fact, we can conclude that other interventions of a similar sort will follow, with little popular opposition, and that the Nixon administration may succeed in carrying out its intended "low-cost, long-haul" strategy in Indochina, maintaining the technological war at its present phenomenal level while relying, to the extent that it can, on native troops armed, led, supplied, trained, and backed by Americans.

It is important to bear in mind that this is the general pattern of military conquest, colonial or otherwise. The Russians do not use the Soviet Army directly to enforce order in Czechoslovakia, and even the Nazis relied largely on native forces to control the occupied territories of Europe. What is unusual about the American war is the inability to create a native structure that has sufficient legitimacy to control the domestic population. It is this deficiency that Nixon hopes to remedy, while maintaining the attack on Indochina at its present massive scale. And so long as the debate here turns solely on the question of "cost," this strategy may succeed in imposing the rule of the elites that the U.S. defends, a bitter tragedy for the peasant societies of Indochina. There is a great deal more to say about this matter, but this is not the place, and I will therefore drop the matter here, merely reiterating that I do not think that one can object to the Berrigans' actions on the grounds that the American intervention is legitimate, though perhaps unwise.

OPPOSITION TO A "DEMOCRATIC" WAR

One who agrees with this judgment will naturally turn to the question whether civil disobedience is an appropriate form of opposition to the war, in a democracy. Several issues are intermingled here. Suppose, for the sake of argument, that the U.S. were a perfectly functioning democracy, and that our policy in Indochina had been determined by an informed electorate, through the democratic process. Would it then follow that civil disobedience is illegitimate? The answer is, surely, that it would not follow from these assumptions alone. There is no principle that supports the conclusion that the people of Indochina must be subjected to a criminal attack, if the American people so determine by exercise of their democratic rights. There is no principle from which it follows that a pure, unflawed democratic society must be permitted to continue tranquil and undisturbed, while it carries out criminal actions.

Rather, citizens of this society (under the circumstances we have postulated) are faced with a dilemma, a conflict of principles: on the one hand, there is the commitment to the democratic process; on the other, a commitment to save Vietnam (and Laos, and now perhaps Cambodia) from extinction as a cultural and historic entity, or simply to defend them from criminal attack. One has to weigh these conflicting principles, and determine which is overriding, under the circumstances. But this question leads us back, immediately, to the issue of the legitimacy and character of the American intervention. It seems to me that an objective and reasoned evaluation of the circumstances and historical facts leads to the conclusion that civil disobedience would be legitimate, even on the assumption that our policies in Indochina were the expression of the will of the people in a perfectly functioning democracy.

OPPOSITION TO AN "EXECUTIVE" WAR

However, the assumption is quite unacceptable. I shall not discuss here the inevitable limitations on democracy under a highly centralized, militarized state capitalist system of the contemporary American variety. But consider the determination of policy in a narrower sense. In November 1964, the population voted overwhelmingly against the policies which were put into effect immediately after the election, policies which, it appears, had been proposed unanimously by the President's advisors even prior to the election, though the electorate was never so informed.

Or consider Laos. The American bombardment of Laos began in May, 1964, and has continued without let-up since. The bombing was sharply escalated in 1968, and again in 1969, and has reached levels of intensity that have few, if any, historical parallels. The bombardment is largely directed against the civil society administered by the Pathet Lao. Virtually every town, village, and farm has been destroyed in vast areas of the country. Despite massive "population removal" (e.g., from the Plain of Jars), more than a third of the population still lives in these areas, according to American government sources. From direct reports of refugees, now rotting in miserable camps in the areas still under American (i.e., Royal Lao Government) control, and from the direct testimony of reporters who have visited the zones administered by the Pathet Lao, we can reconstruct the story of these years. We know, for example, that tens of thousands, and very likely hundreds of thousands of people are living in caves and tunnels, unable to farm, rarely seeing the light of day, often unable even to escape into the open air at night, because of the intensive bombardment, with its heavy component of anti-personnel weapons and napalm.

What does this have to do with the state of American democracy? The answer is quite simple. All of this has been done in secret. Even Senator Symington, with his close contacts with the Air Force, has stated in Congressional Hearings (Fall, 1969), that he was unaware of what was happening in Laos (in particular, of the unilateral American escalation under the Nixon administration). When he visited the country, he was simply deceived by the Embassy officials and the American military. Such trickery is common when Congressmen visit. Even the Senate Foreign Relations Committee did not know of this executive war. Furthermore, it still does not know; or at least, Administration lies went unchallenged in the Laos Hearings. For example, the Administration claimed that the bombing has been directed against military targets, although the evidence is absolutely overwhelming that a primary target has been the civil society, the socio-economic structure in which the Pathet Lao revolution is rooted. What is hidden from the Senate Foreign Relations Committee is, needless to say, hardly common knowledge in the population at large. It takes immense effort to discover what the U.S. is doing in Laos. Under these circumstances, it is rather pointless to talk about interfering with the democratic process through civil disobedience. The democratic process has been undermined, severely, by the executive branch of the government.

One of the most careful and informed students of executive decision-making in Indochina, Daniel Ellsberg (formerly of the RAND Corporation), testified before Congress in May, 1970, that American "policy has, in fact, been far more knowing, and one would have to say cynical, to insiders, in its contravention of the [Geneva] accord and of our announced goals of self-determination, than an outsider would easily imagine." As an outsider, I can only report that the cynicism of the American executive in Indochina for the past twenty years has few historical parallels, the war in Laos being perhaps the most striking example. The fact that Congress has virtually abandoned its constitutional role is no reason for citizens to tolerate, submissively, the further erosion of democracy. If civil disobedience can effectively curb the lawless and largely secret actions of the executive, then it seems to me a proper course of action.

IMPACT OF PROTEST ON PUBLIC OPINION

This leads us to the next, and, in my opinion most crucial issue. What has been the impact of various types of protest and resistance since 1965, when dissent rose beyond a murmur? Here we must separate two factors: what is the effect on decision-making? what is the effect on public opinion? These do not necessarily correlate. For example, it is possible that some action might lead to a decision to restrict American military involvement, and at the same time to increased public support for this involvement. I doubt that this has happened, though a superficial interpretation of certain facts to which I return might lead one to a different conclusion; but it is certainly a possibility. In any event, the two factors will, obviously, be kept separate by one who wishes to save Indochina from the consequences of our "strategic logic," or from the fate of which Fall warned. Such a person will want to influence public attitudes on the war, and to persuade the public that the American intervention is illegitimate; but, far more important, he will want to modify the decisions taken by the executive in its pursuit of the twenty-year goal of subjugating Indochina—a goal, incidentally, which persists, so far as I can see, despite the public relations efforts of the Nixon administration.

Judgments about the impact of dissent, in either respect, can only be tentative and impressionistic. Occasionally, someone close to the formation of policy gives a glimpse of what he believes to have been operative considerations. For the most part, one must try to reconstruct from very partial evidence. As far as public attitudes are concerned, even less is known. What evidence there is, is rather meaningless. For example, it appears that the short-term effect of mass demonstrations is to antagonize those segments of the population that would prefer not to be disturbed; hence the President's popularity is likely to rise after any action that increases the visibility of the war.

The real question, however, is quite different: what would public attitudes be if the war in Vietnam were not continually forced to consciousness by such actions, if the war were as "invisible" to an apathetic public as the secret executive war in Laos of the past six years? What would have been the possibilities for persuasion, for debate, for discussion of the issues, had mass actions not focused attention on the war, while deepening the commitment of those who participated in them? There has been no systematic investigation of such questions —the only important ones. In fact, it is not at all clear how they could be systematically studied. My own impression, based largely on extensive speaking to quite a wide variety of audiences over the years, is that mass demonstrations have been a major factor in bringing the war to public attention, and that resistance, particularly draft resistance, has had an appreciable effect in bringing many people to examine their own complicity and

to draw them to the kinds of actions that have influenced policymakers.

In some cases, it is clear that protest and resistance have had dramatic, if small-scale effects. My
own university, M.I.T., can serve as an example. In
1965–66, there was little interest in the war. Teach-
ins drew small groups, often antagonistic. In fact,
M.I.T. students were prominently engaged in violent
disruptions of public meetings against the war. The
mood slowly changed as the war continued, but a
really dramatic change was caused by a sanctuary
for an A.W.O.L. soldier in the fall of 1968. Not
only did this draw great numbers of apathetic or
hostile students into a serious consideration of the
issues (hence, as usual, to strong and principled
opposition to the war), but it also set the stage for
the first, very belated critical inquiry, by the faculty
and student body, into university complicity in the
military enterprises of the state. Many similar examples can be cited.

IMPACT OF PROTEST ON POLICY

Consider the question of the impact on policy.
What, for example, was the effect of domestic protest on the rejection of Westmoreland's demand for
two hundred thousand additional troops after the
Tet offensive? or on Nixon's turn to the strategy of
a long-haul, low-cost war? or on the extent of the
Cambodian invasion? or on the decision to refrain
from bombing the center of Hanoi and Haiphong,
along with the rest of the country, which was devastated?

We can make some educated guesses. Townsend
Hoopes' interesting memoirs indicate that the oper-

ative domestic factor in post-Tet planning was protest and resistance, the fear that American society
would become ungovernable (There were of course
other factors, such as the international monetary
crisis that threatened, if the war were to be further
escalated). Hoopes reports that his own opposition
to escalation, even continuation of the war, was
based in large part on his belief that it would lead
to renewed demonstrations, draft resistance, domestic turmoil, bitterness and alienation of the young.
Others who have been close to the formation of
policy have spoken in similar terms.

This is important evidence; it strongly supports
the judgment that mass protest and resistance have
been a major factor in bringing about the changes
of tactics in executive policy in recent years. Thus
the timing of Nixon's November 3, 1969, announcement of troop withdrawals, as well as its content
and manner, strongly suggest that this was an effort
to respond to (and defuse) the massive fall demonstrations; or, in other words, that the fall
actions were the immediate cause of this tactical
adjustment. A comparison of Nixon's television
performance announcing the Cambodian invasion
with his second appearance, a week later, as he
sought desperately to build bridges to the young,
certainly suggests that the spontaneous student
strike was a factor in limiting the plans for the
invasion of Cambodia (what they may have been,
we can only guess and may never know). The
secrecy and endless deception of the executive is
itself a clear indication of its fear of public response to the actual facts of the war it is waging
in Indochina.

There is direct testimony, occasionally, that gives
some insight into how the executive hopes to "pac-

ify" the American population. For example, Secretary of the Army Resor, testifying before Congress a year ago, said that "if we can just buy some time in the United States by these periodic progressive withdrawals and the American people can just shore up their patience and determination, I think we can bring this to a successful conclusion"—a "successful conclusion" that may very well be the final conclusion of our strategic logic. It is mass protest and resistance that have, over the years, prevented the executive from "buying time" for its various designs, and created a mood of concern in which the deceptions of the government, and the facts of the situation, can be brought to the consciousness of at least a part of the population.

No one would argue that every antiwar action has been effective either in combatting the general passivity that permits the war-makers to act freely or in increasing the level of opposition to the war. However, it seems fairly clear that, had it not been for the mass actions of protest and the determined resistance of a few, the scale and intensity of the American war in Southeast Asia would have been even more ferocious than what we have seen in the past years, and the general public (including, incidentally, the "academic community," which has generally been roused from quiescence only by student activism), though perhaps not enthusiastic, would have persisted in what Hans Morganthau calls "our conformist subservience to state power."

ANDREW GREELEY'S "FACTS"

Andrew Greeley, in his article mentioned earlier, reaches very different conclusions. He claims that the war is ending "not because of the Daniel Berrigans (quite the contrary, the research data suggest that the Berrigans and the rest of the protesting rabble may have prolonged the war) but despite them, because the members of a free and open society have, however belatedly, made it impossible for the government to continue to wage the war." He adds that "this is the first time in the history of the human race that a major power has been forced out of a war simply because its people do not approve of it . . ." The latter statement is clearly untrue. Consider only our predecessors in the effort to maintain Western dominance in Indochina. The French, as Bernard Fall pointed out, "never dared to send conscripts to Viet-Nam, nor did they increase the draft at home for fear of public opposition to the war"—despite their historic "interests" in Indochina. With the "Nixon doctrine," we are beginning to reduce the American commitment to victory to a level that the French government could never achieve, because "its people did not approve of it." Had the French "approved of" the war to the extent that Americans still do, France could also have sent a massive conscript army, though it obviously could not have matched the technological resources with which we batter Indochina.

In passing, I might note that this casual attitude to fact is rather typical of Greeley's political discussions. I have already noted his weird version of the views of the Berrigans. Similarly, in commenting on my views (*New Republic*, June 27, 1970), he speaks of "Professor Chomsky's assertion that we are the most imperialistic country that ever existed, an assertion which has historical problems of its own"—as indeed it does, though they hardly compare to the problem of finding any such assertion, or anything that even vaguely suggests it, in anything that I have ever written or said.

However, despite his carelessness and irresponsibility, it is important to consider seriously his claim that the "protesting rabble" may have prolonged the war. His claim that the "research data" support his view is probably a reference to the fact that polls generally indicate an increase in support for the President after mass demonstrations. I have already pointed out why this is quite meaningless. There are no further "research data," to my knowledge, that suggest anything significant about the effect of mass protest and resistance on public attitudes, and as far as the effect on decision-making is concerned, what evidence there is suggests that mass protest and resistance are precisely what has led to changes of tactics over the years, as I have already noted. But Greeley is on target, more or less, in asserting that it is the public that has "made it impossible for the government to continue to wage the war." To be more accurate, it is certain segments of the public—largely the student movement—that has made it difficult for the government to wage the war with the freedom and abandon it would wish. And this segment of the public, Greeley's "protesting rabble," has been inspired, to a significant extent, by Dan and Phil Berrigan and a few others like them.

On the other hand, if the objects of Greeley's sneering accusations had followed his example (and advice) over the past few years, then it is likely that Bernard Fall's warning would have come much closer to fulfillment and that our strategic logic would have been pursued many steps nearer to its final conclusion. One can debate the exact degree of impact of the actions of the Berrigans and others like them, and the many thousands who have been influenced by their conscientious resistance to rouse themselves from apathy, and to involve themselves in some way in visible opposition to the war.

There is, so far as I can see, no reasonable doubt that mass protest and resistance have been major factors in constraining the executive. And, though the evidence here is less compelling, it seems to me plausible that mass protest and resistance have, over the years, kept the war in the public eye and defeated the efforts to create the atmosphere of conformist subservience that would permit the free exercise of American military power. Whether this will continue to be the case, I cannot say. However, if the "protesting rabble" is silenced, then the Nixon strategy of an unending war of devastation may be pursued to a "successful conclusion," and, at best, the future prospects for the societies of Indochina are dim indeed.

EFFECTS OF THE BERRIGANS' ACTIONS

Such considerations still do not bear on the more specific question of the effects of actions such as the destruction of draft files at Catonsville. Suppose, for example, that one could show that such actions have helped create an atmosphere in which some people have been led to terrorist attacks that are deplorable in themselves, as well as useful only to the government in its efforts to reinforce the conformist subservience to state power. Then,

I believe, one would have to conclude that the draft file destruction was improper, because of its social consequences, even if (as I believe) legitimate in principle. Again, judgments can only be tentative. However, from what information is available to me, I do not believe that actions such as those of the Catonsville Nine and the Milwaukee Fourteen have in any way contributed to terrorism. It might be argued that, had there been a more extensive involvement in nonviolent actions such as those of the Berrigans, then perhaps the mood of desperation that leads some to terrorism might have been abated. I don't know how to evaluate this possibility.

Have the actions of the Berrigans and others led to a heightened consciousness and commitment to oppose the war? There is little doubt of this, though the circles may be small. Have they produced a negative reaction in wider circles, say, a reversion to the kind of authoritarianism that benefits only state power? I know of no reason to believe this. My impression is that actions such as those in Catonsville and Milwaukee might receive broad support, if the effort were made to explain and discuss them. If there has been a serious failing, I think it is in this indispensable second-order effort.

I have not discussed the question of willing submission to state authority. It is often maintained that this is a necessary component of legitimate civil disobedience. I simply do not see the logic of this argument. It seems to me that there is no moral compulsion for one who seeks to prevent criminal actions of the state to submit voluntarily to punishment for his actions. Refusal to submit to punishment does not, in itself, imply a refusal to recognize the general legitimacy of the government (often proposed as the criterion to distinguish civil disobedience from rebellion), just as a refusal to contribute voluntarily to criminal acts by the payment of war taxes does not, in itself, challenge the legitimacy of the government. Rather, it is a challenge to the legitimacy of specific actions taken by what may or may not be a legitimate authority, on other grounds.

There is the more specific question: is it proper to destroy draft files (granted, for the sake of discussion, that all other arguments against such actions have been allayed)? There is no doubt that there is a coercive element in such actions, in that the rights of registrants and the demands on them are affected, without their consent or choice. Furthermore, the effect is not to prevent recruitment for the armed forces, but to redistribute it. One might say the same, in part, about draft resistance, although when the scale becomes significant—as in Northern California, where extremely high rates of refusal to serve are reported, perhaps approaching two thirds—there is a qualitative change in the political impact of the action. There has been a good deal of discussion of these matters, primarily among pacifists, and I have nothing to add. To me it seems that the crucial issue is the impact of such actions on ending the atrocity of the American war. If the contribution is significant, then this more than compensates for the element of coercion which, if we are to be honest, is rarely absent in some form in nonviolent civil disobedience, much as we may and should try to diminish it.

THE WITNESS OF THE BERRIGANS

In discussing the questions raised by the Berrigans' actions I have tried to consider the issues dispassionately. Admittedly, this is difficult. We are not discussing abstract questions of logic, but the fate of a people, the existence of a society.

It is not necessary to visit Indochina to appreciate the horror of the American war. The bare statistics suffice. The tonnage of bombardment is now approaching three times the total expended by the American military in all theaters in World War II. Defoliation has been carried out at high levels of intensity over an area that exceeds that of Massachusetts, more than 10 percent of it crop destruction. The long-term effects can only be guessed. In Cambodia, after only a few months of war, there are an estimated one million refugees out of a poulation of hardly more than six million, not including the half-million Vietnamese who were imprisoned, driven from their homes, and massacred in the thousands by the Cambodian army. Despite government lies, the fact is that intensive American bombardment, by B-52's, Phantoms, helicopter gunships, the whole array of weapons of terror, continues at a high level in Cambodia. In South Vietnam and Laos it is impossible to estimate the number of refugees, but it must be on the order of from a quarter to a third of the population. The American war against the peasant society of Laos —this is the appropriate term—is particularly grotesque. Laos is among the poorest countries of the world. Much of its population does not even know of the existence of Laos, let alone the United

States, the source of the savage attack from privileged sanctuaries in Thailand and the China Sea. Saigon is the most densely populated city in the world; the rural population has been "urbanized" by American bombs and artillery. A careful study by Jonathan Schell showed that one province, Quang Ngai, was 70 percent destroyed by 1967, that is, before the massive escalation of the technological war.

One can continue endlessly with the array of horrors and atrocities. The point is that it is difficult, when one is willing to face the facts, to try to balance properly the legitimate types of disruption against the effects on the people of Indochina of our domestic apathy.

At a lesser scale of intensity, it is difficult to be dispassionate about the Berrigans. No one who knows them can doubt that they are heroic individuals, willing to do what many realize should be done, regardless of the personal cost, with a simplicity of manner and a commitment to principle that can only inspire the deepest respect. There are not too many people of whom this can honestly be said. Andrew Greeley chooses to scoff at the comparison of Dan Berrigan to Dietrich Bonhoeffer. The comparison, however, is quite appropriate.

In a recent article, Richard Falk, Professor of International Law at Princeton, recalled Roosevelt's appeal to the German people:

Hitler is committing these crimes against humanity in the name of the German people. I ask every German and every man everywhere under Nazi domination to show the world that he does not share these insane criminal desires.

He adds: "A similar appeal to the American people by responsible leaders is long overdue." There
has been, and will be no such appeal. There have,
however, been a few men and women who have
shown that they will not be part of the criminal
assault on the people of Indochina. The Berrigans
are among those few.

Robert McAfee Brown

The Berrigans: Signs or Models?

Most of the people writing about the Berrigans these days make a big point of the closeness of their own relationship to one or both of the men who have become such important symbols of war protest, and who will continue to occupy that role even through their years in prison. I had better begin, therefore, by admitting that I can't score many points that way, much as I would like to claim them as close friends. On a few occasions, I appeared on antiwar programs and platforms with one or both of them; I had the privilege of introducing Dan at his last appearance before the Stanford University student body; I also had the privilege of speaking on a program with Phil one summer at Emory University in Atlanta, and exchanged some letters with him after he was first arrested. Since both of them spoke and wrote so much, however, and spoke and wrote with such unforgettable vigor and moral passion, those of us whose personal acquaintance with them has not been of long duration nevertheless feel that we know them very well. By all accounts, this has been true also of those who have only known the Berrigans through books or television. Since both of them have such skill in communicating, Dan through quiet but compelling poetic imagery and Phil through his fact-filled and powerful arguments against the war, their impact in personal terms has surely been much wider than either of them is aware.

Why is this so? Why has the witness of these two men been so widespread and so profound? I think the fundamental reason is that they have served in our war-wracked society as *signs* pointing to some truths we would otherwise forget (and might indeed prefer to ignore) even when they have not always served as *models* whom people have directly imitated. This point came home to me with great vividness after Dan spoke to the Stanford student body shortly after he had been tried and convicted for dropping napalm on draft board records and was awaiting sentence. He described in a very quiet and persuasive way the reasons that led him to take that action, an action that seemed rather strange and perhaps even grotesque to much of his audience. But the morning after his speech, two students with their fiancées appeared in my office, stating that while they were not yet ready to drop napalm on draft board records, they did feel, as one of them put it, that "Father Berrigan has raised the ante for all of us." Both students had been considering requesting classification from their draft boards as conscientious objectors to the war. But after hearing Dan Berrigan, they had to ask themselves whether they could comply even to that extent with a structure that was supplying the manpower to prolong the war. Subsequently, both students decided that they must turn in their draft cards and refuse to be part of the Selective Service System; at this writing they await the inevitable arrest and imprisonment that will come. Dan Berrigan was to them a *sign* if not a model—a sign that things are not well in our society, a sign that each of us is called to move from ordinary to extraordinary action in order to force out society to realign its moral priorities.

Another way in which the Berrigans have served as signs to our society has been by the highly symbolic character of what they have done, creating pictorial images that are uncomfortably difficult to erase from our minds. If their action at Catonsville seemed "grotesque" to some, it also served to dramatize, in unforgettable fashion, the grotesque moral priorities that have been erected in our country: that we give medals to men who drop napalm on civilians in Southeast Asia, but imprison men who drop napalm on pieces of paper in southeast United States. If such a statement seems oversimplified, it is nevertheless a vivid and poignant reminder of what has happened to the collective conscience of our nation: we are outraged when paper is burned, and we are not outraged when children are burned. So when people respond that the action of the Berrigans was "extreme," I think the Berrigans are justified in responding that extreme moral insensitivity on a national scale calls for extreme action on an individual scale to challenge such moral insensitivity: "Our apologies, good friends, for the fracture of good order, the burning of paper instead of children, the angering of the orderlies in the front parlor of the charnel house. We could not, so help us God, do otherwise. For we are sick at heart, our hearts give us no rest from thinking of the Land of Burning Children." So wrote Daniel in the preface to *Night Flight to Hanoi*.

I do not think the Berrigans have suggested that their action at Catonsville was a *model* for everyone else. But I think they have demonstrated that their action is a *sign* to everyone else, namely a sign that our country has dislocated its sense of right and wrong, and that when the rest of us remain insensitive to that dislocation, ways must be found to bring us to our senses and restore our moral sensibilities. If we do not drop napalm, then we must find *our own ways* to get the message across to others. Until we do, the Berrigans will give us no rest.

"WHO IS TRULY FREE?"

Another way in which the Berrigans have been a sign to our society is epitomized by the astonishing photograph that appeared in the national press on the morning after Dan's arrest. It was the epitome of the nature of our contemporary society. For here were two men, one of them smiling, free, and clearly liberated, the other scowling, uptight, and clearly in bondage. But it was not the F.B.I. agent who was free; the free man was Daniel. And it was not Daniel who was in bondage; the man in bondage was the F.B.I. agent. So one looked at this picture and asked, "Who is truly free?" And the answer was that the man who was going to prison was the man who was truly free, while the man who was sending him to prison was the man who was truly bound. All the normal assessments of our society were challenged by the spontaneous gaiety of a man about to spend three and one-half years in jail.

Let us press the point. What is the power of their

witness? Why have we continued to listen to them? Why have we felt a strange wistfulness that they have been doing things that needed to be done even if we ourselves were not doing them? Why is it likely to be the case that when the history of the twentieth-century church is written, the Berrigans, both of them "criminals" in the ordinary sense of the word, may be remembered as the truly prophetic witnesses of our time? I think the answer is found in the remarkably high degree of consistency between their words and their deeds. They said what many of us said, but they then went on to do what few of us were willing to do, putting themselves in total jeopardy for the sake of their convictions. And each acted on his own style. Dan, as many have commented, has something of the pixie in him, and he is a poet, whatever else he may be as a politician and an activist. Phil is strong on well-documented sledgehammer analysis, and yet he does not let analysis go bail for action. Both of them, in other words, converged from different perspectives on the need to do and not merely to say. And it is surely the nature of the prophet that he acts out what he believes, and does not merely talk about it, even when the action will entail the payment of a heavy price.

Such commitment is the more compelling when seen within the framework of other commitments already made. I am impressed, for example, by their mutual pledge to one another that they would not leave the Roman Catholic priesthood. It has become far too easy for Christians, and especially Catholics, to "write off" the more *avant-garde* social witness of those Catholics who have subsequently left the church. But the Berrigans are not going to give us such an easy out, and they will be around to haunt those of us who are part of the Christian community for many years to come.

A final factor that gives power to their witness is the fact that their minds—and deeds—have not remained static. Both of them have moved long strides from where they originally started, one step at a time, and each advance a decisive one. They have not been content to "do their thing" in ordinary, conventional fashion, do it over and over again, complain about not being heard, and let it go at that. This, I fear, has been the route for most of the rest of us. Instead, as they have seen one level of protest after another fail to make an impact on the American conscience, they have been willing to move to new forms of protest. As they have moved to higher degrees of protest, they have had a smaller constituency following them in every detail. But each advance in their thinking and acting has forced the rest of us to re-examine our own thinking and acting. They have made it impossible for the rest of us to be content with where we are. They continue, as my student commented, "to raise the ante for all of us."

All who were present at the time of the trial in Baltimore will testify that both brothers spent inordinate amounts of time outside of court urging their supporters to cool it, to avoid inciting violence or provoking it, insisting at every turn that the way to make a witness against violence in Southeast Asia was hardly to practice violence in southeast America. Any attempt to equate the Berrigan actions with the violence-prone activities of the militant far left is surely stretching the facts further than the truth will bear. And if there has been any single point at which the sign-model analysis is to be faulted, it is surely at this point—that nonviolence is an increasingly compelling *model* for producing social change, thanks particularly to the Berrigans, as well as Martin Luther King, Cesar Chavez, Archbishop Helder Camara and a few others. There is a difference between the revolutionary who wants to bomb, burn, and destroy, and the revolutionary who proposes to bring about change through means other than bombing, burning, and destroying. The latter is the vocation the Berrigan brothers have taken upon themselves, and one must hope that even from their pulpits in prison, they can continue to make us hear the reality that, at least for those of us who are white, middle-class Americans, a peculiar burden of witness is placed upon us to engage in the changing of our society by means that are nonviolent.

SOME PROBLEMS THE BERRIGANS BEQUEATH TO US

A variety of questions can be raised about the place of the Berrigans on the American scene.

1. We must continually ask ourselves why we are so attracted to them when we hear what they say and yet do not do the things they do. There is a terrible temptation to let them go bail for us, to say in effect that because they have done what they did, we need do nothing more. We are tempted to take refuge in that fact that because they have been a sign, we need not be, or to be content with the fact that since they are in jail, the witness has been made (by somebody else, thank God) and we are thus let off the hook. It may be that we are attracted to them precisely because the level of their commitment is so much deeper than ours that we never feel really threatened by their presence into

doing deeds that could bring similar unfortunate consequences upon ourselves.

2. Their actions highlight an on-going perplexity in the realm of ethics: do we act as we do (a) simply because we must, whatever the consequences, or (b) are we called upon to weigh the consequences in deciding what we will do? The great danger in adopting the latter alternative is that we will always back off from decisive action because the consequences might be other than we desire, or are so unclear that we cannot weigh what their implications might be. But there comes a point in the lives of all of us when we simply must act on the basis of that great Catholic principle, "Here I stand, I can do no other." Dan and Phil clearly reached that point long ago, I believe, and they clearly believe also that the consequences of their actions will help, rather than hinder, the cause of peace. But what if this assessment turns out to be incorrect? What if the consequences should turn out to be (as the saying goes) counterproductive? As we have already seen, some argue that in doing what they did the Berrigans have made it more difficult to end the war by stirring up protest not against the war but against the protestors against the war.

The difficulty with this argument, as already suggested, is that since one can never be sure of all the consequences, and since baleful ones can always be projected, one may be reduced to such a vapid kind of moderation that no significant prophetic stance is ever taken. No one would be happier than Mr. Agnew or Mr. Mitchell if all those against the war never acted in a way that could produce counterrelations in "middle America." If one does not risk stirring up antagonism, one simply allows apathy or injustice to reign unchallenged. When one recalls the statements that Mr. Nixon, Mr. Agnew, and Mr. Mitchell have made about protest and dissent in the last twelve months, it is clear that they are prepared to allow any kind of "dissent" that does not threaten their own policy in Southeast Asia. Any significant action will carry within it the risk of stirring up antagonism, but it can also carry within it the possibility of creating new centers of support, and even through the antagonism helping to join the issue in a way that would have been impossible otherwise. So against the charge that certain types of actions may have unfortunate consequences can be offered the counter-charge that inaction may have the most unfortunate consequences of all.

3. An even tougher question raised by the Berrigans' activities is that of the degree of allegiance one is called upon to give to a structural fabric in our society. (I use the words "structural fabric" as a rather awkward circumlocution for "law and order," since the latter has come to be such a code word for right-wing oppression.) When the Berrigans first burned the draft-board records, they waited for the police to arrest them, submitted to trial and indicated that they would go to jail if convicted. But somewhere along the line, they came to the conclusion that it was no longer proper to play ball with the system, and that a corrupt society had no claim over their consciences. Now *any* Christian must affirm that a point may come when he must refuse to play ball with the system. Many of us have been far less vigorous in our war-protest activities than the Berrigans have asserted that at certain points we are willing to break the law, but very few of us

have challenged the whole legal system to the extent exemplified by the Berrigans' evasion of arrest. A sick society needs some kind of order and structure, and one must analyze the social structures very carefully before deciding that a given society is beyond repair from within.

Such a point of total defiance clearly arrived for Dietrich Bonhoeffer and his collaborators in their resistance against Nazi Germany, and it has always been a part of Christian belief that in the final analysis, "We must obey God, rather than men." (Acts 5:29) Whether we can maintain the minimal structures necessary for social life without allegiance to some system of law, and without courts and punishment for the breaking of law, is a question that the Berrigans force us to consider afresh, and their actions provide a disturbing sign that we must take seriously, particularly if those actions are not yet the model most of us are prepared to imitate.

(My existential confusion is symbolized by the fact that I took a kind of unholy glee in the fact that Daniel Berrigan was able to elude the oh-so-efficient F.B.I. for four months, even though I would not take that course of action if I myself were arrested, convicted, and sentenced to jail. Perhaps my glee was irresponsibly romantic, the comfortable glee of one who enjoys seeing *somebody else* demythologize an omnipotent power, and is willing to let somebody else pay the price for one's own greater sense of freedom. But Dan has reminded me by his action that there is a kind of liberty that is possible even when one is bound, a kind of liberty than can be exercised even by those who are being hunted and pursued. And in this very uptight age, that is a lesson all of us need to learn.)

CONCLUSION

Signs or models? The Berrigans are a legitimate prophetic sign to us so long as we do not let their actions go bail for our inactions, and they will remain an ongoing prophetic sign by continually keeping us off balance, as their very absence from our immediate midst forces us continually to re-evaluate the kind of society that brands them criminals. But if they *free* us to make our own protests in our own ways, they also *bind* us to make those protests more sharply tomorrow than we did yesterday, and to face the uncomfortable possibility that what we may be called upon to do next week is of a magnitude we would not even have considered last month.

David J. O'Brien

The Berrigans and America

Daniel Berrigan, S.J., and Philip Berrigan, S.S.J., today are in Danbury Federal Prison, convicted of violation of federal statutes for their participation in the destruction of Selective Service records on May 17, 1968. Although they pleaded innocent at their trial, they freely admitted that they had committed the acts in question. They are criminals, of that there can be no doubt; "criminals for peace," as they see it, decent and sincere men who simply broke the law, as the trial judge saw it. At first they had expected and welcomed the prospect of jail. "We stayed and were taken," Daniel Berrigan wrote, "because we believe our society and our church have no need of a romantic hit-and-run underground. The need is for at least a few who will act on behalf of public decency and pay up, as I believe Christian and Gandhian ethics demand." Later, arguing that "the courts have become more and more the instruments of the war-makers," they concluded that the entire judicial system lacked moral and legal justification. They therefore evaded arrest and were jailed only after pursuit by federal authorities.

The Berrigans see themselves, and are seen by

their admirers, as prisoners for conscience, men jailed for exercising their basic right to follow their convictions. For others, Daniel Berrigan is, like his brother and friends, "a moral zealot," even "a self-righteous fanatic." The strength of the emotions revealed in this controversy reached new heights when the Justice Department charged Philip Berrigan with masterminding a plot to blow up Washington steam tunnels and kidnap White House aide Henry Kissinger; Daniel Berrigan was named as a co-conspirator. These new charges brought the Berrigans and their ideas to the attention of a far greater segment of the American public than they had been able to reach themselves and generated new debate about these radical priests and the war they have sworn to resist. In this respect at least the Catonsville draft-board raiders accomplished their purpose, for, as Thomas Melville put it at the trial, the defendants asked "only that America consider seriously the points we have tried to raise."

The Vietnam war is not the first event in American history to occasion such protests and the Berrigans are not the first Americans to find dramatic methods of confronting the government and awakening the conscience of their fellow citizens. Colonial patriots, opponents of slavery, labor organizers, suffragettes, radicals and pacifists, all broke American laws and appealed to a "higher law" for justification, which meant in effect appeal to the conscience of the people. Deliberate law breaking is not foreign to Christian history either, for laymen and clergy in most western nations at some time in their history have felt compelled by circumstances or conviction to oppose the state, to suffer imprisonment, or to become fugitives. Judgment of these earlier rebels is relatively easy, for we believe that they resisted in circumstances much different from our own (for example, Nazi Germany). Many rebels who suffered for a cause which later proved victorious in the struggle of history are enshrined as national or religious heroes. In addition, we usually envision yesterday's rebels as resisters of active, repressive power. Even if we do not practice pacifism and civil disobedience, we can and do respect its adherents: a Thoreau, a Dorothy Day, or a Martin Luther King. At one time the Berrigans fit this mold. When Daniel Berrigan was sent out of the country in 1965 in an apparent effort to stifle his antiwar activity, or when his brother Philip was transferred from Newburg, New York to appease right-wing Catholics, they enjoyed widespread sympathy and considerable support. But their actions in 1968 shattered that support, for then they moved beyond a simple pacifism of protest and dissent to active, militant resistance. Earlier they had insisted on the obligation of Christians to work against war and racism, a call sufficiently familiar to raise no great commotion. After all, the church and the nation had always had its share of well-intentioned, if naïve, idealists. After Catonsville the challenge of the Berrigans went much deeper, their demands became much greater, and their enemies became much more powerful, determined, and ruthless.

It is altogether too easy to underestimate how serious and difficult a path the Berrigans are following. Many call them "prophets," an accurate enough designation but one which allows others to evade their own personal responsibility, for most people feel that the prophet belongs to a special class of men chosen by God for an unusual mission. The prophet should be listened to with great seriousness, but not necessarily heeded, much less imitated. Others emphasize that the Berrigans are priests, exercising a "new ministry" somehow emanating from the ecclesiastical changes of the second Vatican Council. In this view their clerical vocation is a special one, which requires them to teach in a dramatic and personally hazardous fashion. But the layman, or the parish priest for that matter, has other responsibilities to take account of. Called to a different vocation, he must take the Catonsville action with the same seriousness he gives to the pastoral advice of his bishop or the sermon of a visiting priest noted for his holiness and dedication. These images do less than justice to the claims which Daniel and Philip Berrigan have made. Those very workaday responsibilities of job and family which compel a moderate response to the radical evil of our times are for the Berrigans the very heart of the problem, for these commitments to comfort, security, and success cut us off from the poor, the oppressed, and the innocent victims of American military power. In the vision of the new Catholic radicals, it is our involvement in private affairs which prevents us from living the Christian life for others and allows those who possess the reins of power to systematically destroy people in every nation who struggle for freedom, dignity, and justice.

As a result, the Berrigans summon their fellow Americans to what *Commonweal* describes as "a moral revolution, a regeneration that is based on the personal conversion of individuals through acts which break them off from established powers of the world and which link them, through suffering and the fate of being outcast, with the poor and the oppressed." All of America, its governments and courts, its businesses and unions, its churches and its schools are implicated in the evils of war and oppression. All of us are implicated, not simply to the degree that we refuse to act publicly to correct these things, but to the degree that we refuse to cut ourselves off from the jobs, the associations, the goods and services we enjoy in this country, and to the degree that we do not aid, abet, or imitate the actions of the Berrigans and their colleagues in the resistance. How are we Christians to formulate a responsible position in the face of the terribly crucial questions which the Berrigans raise? Part of the answer must lie within each of us, in the inner depths of our conscience where we make those crucial decisions which determine the character of our lives. There are those who regard this as the only relevant arena of decision: what really matters is the inner commitment to love, to a life for others, to the suffering people of the world. But this argument suggests a rejection of intellect and abhorrence for a reasonable assessment of consequences which easily leads to fanaticism. Our decision to disrupt a draft board or bomb a building or quit a job might help end the war and save thousands of Vietnamese lives. It might just as easily deepen national divisions, harden the hearts of many in and out of government, prolong the war, and occasion new wars at home and abroad. Free, responsible, and therefore morally meaningful, decisions require careful analysis and judgment. This in turn requires an effort to define what our Christianity means for us. Here we are on our own, for no question more severely divides the churches than that of the social and political implications of Christian commitment. Equally important, we must formulate a judgment about American conditions and how they can be changed.

It is not too much to say that on this last level, in the assessment of America as it is, the most significant developments have taken place in the position of the Berrigans and hundreds like them. Certainly there has been little if any change in their central commitments or in their belief about Christian responsibility. What has changed is their view of America, the gradual transformation of an almost naïve faith in the goodness of America, and the ability of its people to live up to its ideals, to a shocked awareness of the scandalous failure of the nation to overcome its moral contradictions. One sensitive observer of the Catonsville trial, noting the life history described by each of the accused, concluded "that the defendants might have just as readily led the lives they had selected and for which they had been trained—nurse, teacher, priest, missionary, even the life of the struggling artist— if it were not for the times we live in."

All at Catonsville had, like the Berrigans, dedicated their lives to active service to others, to ending racial and economic injustice and building a new church to aid mankind in its quest for freedom, dignity and justice. All were led by the events of the sixties to drastically alter their assessment of the American context of this commitment and this work. "It is not a time for building justice," Philip Berrigan said, "it is a time for confronting injustice." By 1968 they had concluded that Americans who truly believed in the nation's ideals could only act on their beliefs by resisting the nation's institutions, by being willing "to be accounted a felon," by making the central commitment to "Say NO!"

In a sense, then, the problem posed by the Ber-

rigans is less one of Christian than of American
responsibility. It was not the message of Pope
John XXIII or the Vatican Council which turned
liberal Catholic idealists into militant advocates
of revolution and evangelical preachers of judgment and regeneration. The personal history of
Catholic radicals has been made tortuous not by
any uncertainty about their own values or faith but
by doubt about their country. Marjorie Melville,
former missionary sister and now a convict, put the
matter clearly: "I'm searching for answers to my
question," she told the Catonsville court. "I'm looking for ways to make my country a land of brotherhood, to help it contribute to world peace." Deeply,
even desperately, the Berrigans want the American
people and the American government to live up to
their professed ideals. "Lead us!", Philip Berrigan
cried out to the nation's leaders. "Lead us by giving
people justice and there will be no need to break
the law." If "the system" is reformable, he continued, "Reform it and we will help with all our
conviction and energy in jail or out."

For the members of the resistance, it is America,
not Christianity, which they have tried and found
wanting. In this they reflect the historical experience of the Catholic community from which so
many resisters come. Until very recently American
Catholics considered themselves members of a distinctive minority group outside the mainstream of
American life. This country was for most of its
history predominantly Protestant. Members of Protestant churches filled key posts in government and
business; they set the social and cultural tone of the
nation, and many of them disliked the Catholic
religion and, to a less extent, Catholics themselves.
In response Catholics proclaimed their uncritical

acceptance of the basic values of the country: personal liberty, democratic government, equality of opportunity and material success, while regarding official agencies of the society with suspicion. The public school seemed an agent of Protestant proselytization or religious indifferentism. The universities were seedbeds of alien and unchristian philosophies which threatened to sap the strength not only of Catholic students but of the whole nation. Even the federal government—which enacted prohibition and immigrant exclusion laws, refused to condemn the Ku-Klux Klan and flirted with the anti-Catholic governments of Mexico and Soviet Russia—seemed hostile to Catholicism. Church leaders, while enthusiastically endorsing the nation's wars, nevertheless often regarded the nation's leaders as unsafe and tried hard to restrict the power of the federal government in national life.

Conservative bishops even endorsed conscientious objection in the late 1930's and opposed universal military training in the 1940's. It was liberal Catholics, emancipated from minority fears and ghetto attitudes, who uncritically championed the growth of federal power and sought to overcome the hostility of respectable non-Catholics by backing mainstream liberal politics, including the basic tenets of the Cold War. The gradual triumph of their views culminated in the election of John Kennedy which ended the period of isolation and removed the final barriers which had prevented Catholic Americanism from identifying with the federal government and its policies. The Vatican Council's Declaration on Religious Liberty and its new spirit of openness and freedom completed the process. The Catholic was now fully American and he and his church were important, respected participants in American life.

Nevertheless, many American Catholics today are experiencing a serious crisis of identity. Part of this crisis derives from the changes initiated by the Vatican Council. Catholics in America had known themselves as Christians who were required to attend church on Sunday, to refrain from eating meat on Friday, to support parochial schools and oppose birth control and dirty movies. All these things were called into question by changes in church discipline and atmosphere in the 1960's, at the same time that changes in theology, liturgy, and relations with other churches were transforming Catholic life and thought. While the loyalty of many Catholics easily weathered the storm, a significant number found it impossible to continue in older roles and adopted a far more informal relationship to the church than would have been thought permissible a few years ago. Most important, the parish, which provided for generations a meaningful structure for worship, education, social life, and service to the community exerted little attraction for younger Catholics maturing in this decade.

At the same time that the Catholic side of American Catholicism was changing, America itself was experiencing the profound shocks that would push the Berrigans to Catonsville and prison. In the 1960's young Catholics, their desire for service fired by the black revolution and the models offered by men like Robert Kennedy, no longer experienced the economic and social pressures which had always forced minority groups to accommodate to American realities. In this situation there was an obvious need for alternatives to the older forms of Christian identification and the older outlets for service to others. In the Kennedy years the option was often the nation itself. How could one better fulfill the functions of the older parish, contact with community, and service to others than through active involvement in programs for social betterment? John Kennedy set the tone in his appeal for public service embodied most significantly in the Peace Corps, while the civil-rights movement provided innumerable opportunities for meaningful work for others. In the mid-sixties the war on poverty opened up thousands of jobs in education and community action, offering outlets for the talent, enthusiasm, and idealism of the young.

It didn't work. Part of the reason lay in the inherent weaknesses of the programs themselves, part in the incredible bureaucratic mazes which confounded workers in the field. Most important, events called into question the seriousness of national commitments. Locally, entrenched powers fought against real change, while nationally funds dried up and moral leadership evaporated. On top of it all came the war, which sharply challenged the integrated Christian Americanism which had been completed in the years since World War II. The war made a mockery of a Christian identity forged around service to fellow man through American institutions. Indeed, the Vietnam war and the events accompanying it destroyed for many the moral authority and credibility of almost every institution which could provide a context for finding meaning, identity, and useful work. The government, once the apparent agent of democratic progress, now seems the purveyor of massive oppression, which in the form of the draft immediately impinges on the young. The churches seem so compromised by their respectability or so internally divided that they can provide no locus of meaningful commitment. The university's service to the nation has made of it an agent of the government's no longer beneficent purposes. Even social-service agencies which work for the poor seem simply to put bandaids on the cancers of American society. Where is one to turn in this situation, to find community, to serve one's fellow men, to worship God with others?

It is just this vacuum in the lives of people who are real, warm human beings that the Berrigans and others like them are trying to fill. "I sense . . . a personal and public malaise, running deep and hard," Daniel Berrigan writes. "More people than we readily imagine have reached a stalemate of such proportions as chill the joy and assail the integrity of marriage, work, religion, education of children, the direction and meaning of life itself." For the Berrigans theirs can no longer be, if it ever was, simply a personal witness against injustice. When all that was needed was the personal sacrifice of a few to arouse public opinion, the Berrigans were confident, sure of themselves, transparently courageous. But if that has failed, if they can no longer hope for quick and decisive public action, then their task has become immeasurably more difficult. Then they must build a movement, communities of men and women finding together not only ways to work to end the war but ways to preserve their sanity and find some joy, some fellowship, some communion with others. From converting the church they must turn to rebuilding it amid its ashes; from saving America they must turn to making it over; from offering themselves as witnesses against evil, they must offer themselves as agents of rebuilding. Daniel and Philip Berrigan have thus become crucially important to the non-violent antiwar movement; many of whose members, might, without their support and example, in one way or another, have destroyed themselves in despair and hatred. They are equally important for many troubled Americans in their suburban living rooms, anguished by the crisis of their nation and even of their family but unable or unwilling themselves to confront the state or to accept the terrible burden thrust on decent men in an era of illegitimate, lawless power.

It is Daniel Berrigan, with his poetic insight and vision, who understands and articulates the subtle shifts in the needs of our people. "Even good people are quite generally resigned to endure a great worsening and rotting of the public fabric," he writes. "But what might it mean to weave a new fabric of life into a new garment, of such cunning and beauty that the wearer himself is transformed by putting it on; from beggar, outcast, bankrupt, alien, loser, prevaricator, imperialist, racist, exploiter—into a new man?" At one and the same time he tells us, it is necessary "to pull the mask of legitimacy from the inhuman and blind face of power" and "to bring a larger community of resistance into being."

The political implications of this position are far from clear or simple. The first requirement is that people "take control of their own lives," recognize their responsibilities and decide to act upon them. For some this may mean development of a new "life style of resistance" in new communities of committed men and women who try to find together ways of living authentically in everyday life the values they have long professed. Equally important, as Philip Berrigan has recognized, "taking control" of life requires a concrete political commitment whose center is the struggle of oppressed people for liberation from the control of illegitimate power. The experience of recent years has led men like Philip Berrigan to the conclusion that the struggle for liberation is going to be a long one, that it demands a more realistic strategy geared to both immediate needs and long-range goals, and that it requires as well work on two fronts: educational work to encourage people to take concrete steps to assume responsibility for their lives and their world, and political work to effectively assist in ending the war, reversing national policy, and supporting the programs of the poor and the oppressed. Gradually the Catholic resistance moves from the clear-cut tasks of denouncing evils and witnessing to the truth to the far more complex and ambiguous effort to bring about fundamental changes in the structure and spirit of American life.

In this context, the actions of the Berrigans at Catonsville and in flight, their marvelous words in which they tell us of the unfolding of their hearts, are signs of hope and not despair, of life and not of death, of reason and not fanaticism. If, as Philip Nobile wrote a few weeks before Daniel's capture, he now seems less sure of himself, less certain that he has the answers, the reason may be that he has turned from resistance to revolution, from "saying no" to the evil of the present to saying yes to the promise of the future. In the difficult and ambiguous effort to build new communities and transform the heart and life of America the Berrigans have much to offer: a vision of better days, an appeal to our best values and traditions, and a strategy which is principled and consistent. While others may differ with their assessment of American society and with the methods of political change that they have chosen, none can avoid the challenge they pose and the responsibility for our country and our fellow man which they thrust on our shoulders.

American radicals from Thomas Jefferson to Martin Luther King stood against prevailing sentiment in the confident expectation that the American people, if they would but see the evil around them, would act to remove it and vindicate their professed ideals. Firmly within this radical tradition, the antiwar movement in its early stages, like the civil-rights movement before it, took the basic decency of the nation and its people for granted. We have only to read the newspaper to know that the loss of that confidence has occasioned the most violent expressions of hatred and despair. Daniel and Philip Berrigan have gone to the edge of that abyss and peered in, and in Daniel's words they have been "stripped naked." They have returned with their spirits intact and their hope unimpaired to summon their fellow Americans to be bold, confident, and faithful. If the shape of the new national community and the tactics and strategy of change remain open, that is the price of our freedom and the weight of our responsibility. What matters now is the decision each of us must make about our own lives, about how we are going to give ourselves, our energies, our talents, and our love in the days ahead. In pressing that decision upon us, the Berrigans are making a difference, even from their prison cells.

John C. Raines

The Followers of Life

In college I was taught to be a political realist. Indeed, for my generation that's what higher education seemed chiefly to mean. At first, of course, there was a kind of sinking feeling. But later came that hard and clever and commanding feeling of knowing how the world "really works." I remember being taught that we had arrived at maturity and so could be trusted as responsible decision-makers when we could look to an election and predict with confidence how various ethnic and socioeconomic status groups would vote their prejudices and narrow self-interests. We lived, we thought, in a stable and trustworthy world, though to be sure a little disappointing. Yet we learned to carry ourselves well in our weighty and unsentimental practicality. We encouraged each other in cultivating our heightened perception of ambiguity, extending and elaborating our sense of special burden in being those who knew the intractable contradictions, cross purposes, and tragedies of life. We enjoyed, in short, our developing aristocracy of soul, our tribal rites of being those who understood and were qualified to steer and intercept the world. As a result, I was quite unprepared for what was to happen.

I think I simply tried to ignore it at first—all these people going to jail. Or perhaps I tried to defend myself by feeling secretly superior to those who had, evidently, not yet learned to live with the more or less continuous tragedy which is human historical existence. Had they not learned about the persistent ways of empires? Had their education to reality failed them so deeply? More likely still, since I too was against the war, I simply questioned the effectiveness of their actions and concluded that, since they were to any objective observer clearly ineffective, they must in fact derive from some other motive than changing the actual circumstances of the world. Likely here was just another instance of the age-old quest for perfection, for self-justification through self-sacrifice, for spiritual ecstasy, martyrdom, and masochism.

But then one day, without my planning or wishing it, I simply found myself in their presence. Some had just returned from federal prison, others were fugitives even then being hunted, still others would soon follow where their friends had gone before. My established universe of reality, which for the past few years had been making increasingly less sense to me, or perhaps I should say within which the sense I could make out of my life was increasingly less satisfying, found itself confronted with a *new definition of reality*. It is to this new perception of man's "real situation in the world" and its relationship to the Berrigan brothers that I want to direct our attention and analysis.

THE RISE OF A NEW CONSCIOUSNESS

It must have come as a gigantic short-circuit to the administrative functionaries of the space program, that they should get shot down by what they put up. It was simply that the most far reaching consequence of their successful efforts remained completely hidden and unanticipated to its technological planners. And that was that man should come to locate himself in reality in a new way. For he began to see himself as seen and define himself as defined in the picture of the earth rising over the desolate deathscape of the moon. To be sure, this is only one way of coming to talk about the new consciousness, one image of its arrival. But it is convenient, and as true as any of the other models of analysis we might also profitably follow.

Man had always been able to take the world for granted. That the future would have a future he could simply assume. It was not a conscious problem or responsibility. But then, after all these millennia of man traveling on, leaving behind him the debris and clutter of his selfishness, mistakes, and tragedies, moving upward and outward in his conquest of the land, his volcanic rise to sovereignty over the earth—suddenly in space he sees himself running out of space. So the short-circuit. Man views himself from the perspective of the moon and realizes to his astonishment that he has only this one human life-space and that the expropriator of the world is in danger of a final expropriation of himself. Put simply, life, at least human life, could no longer be taken for granted.

What an unexpected vision. We had always been able to pursue singlemindedly our narrow projects of living. Success meant success for us and ours: our family, our firm, our social cause, party or nation. So also, defeat and death meant simply that which we had to turn away from our private enclaves of life, directing them instead upon our personal or corporate enemies, upon those who threatened or held back our interests. This was the definition of reality within which we defined our "realisms" and responsible decisions. We wrote it into our philosophies and theologies and psychologies of man. In sociology and political science we elevated it into an "of course" assumption, the taken-for-granted starting point for any serious social analysis. Here, then, was the definition of reality through which we perceived and received ourselves to be in reality. But it was, in fact, a profound and historically relative luxury. And it is this sudden awakening, I believe, that lies close to the heart of the new consciousness and moves the hearts of those like the Berrigan brothers.

The central question of man's life now begins to turn from "how can I make it?" to "can the world make it?" The traditional problem of finding a place in the workaday world is set off balance and complicated by the broader but now equally necessary problem of finding a way to make the world work. Now man has not simply himself and his own on his hands, but the world.

With this new way man has of perceiving his situation in reality, this new consciousness and self-definition, the older realism and responsibility comes to appear insufficiently realistic, indeed fundamentally irresponsible. For that older consciousness could simply take the world and the future for granted and therefore did not need to respond to them as human problems and responsibilities. Rather, the problems needing man's attention were located and defined *within* this wider assumption. We may call it the world-hypothesis of man in free-space competition for survival and preeminence. This realism has now become unreal.

What all of the generations that preceded us in this experiment called man were able simply to assume we can no longer assume. It therefore appears to us that all of the generations which follow us must learn now from our precarious attempts at learning. For it falls now upon each generation to decide whether life shall have life. Each generation, whether it wishes to or not, shall render its concrete actions and priorities either permission or irrevocable denial of the future's hope to be.

It is this new perception of the reality of man's situation which gives rise to the anxious cry that the pacification of human existence become mankind's central project NOW, not as moral fanaticism and self-justification but as a nonnegotiable requirement of the most simple and sober realism. It produces that haunted impatience with promises postponed and traditional values traditionally betrayed for the pursuit of narrow self-interest and gain. It is not that the new generation is better equipped to perceive hypocrisy. Rather, it seems to them that the world can no longer afford what it has always been quite aware of as its own hypocrisy. It is not simply that the problems of scarcity have been potentially overcome, that technology opens up the possibility of a "society beyond necessity." Rather, a new scarcity and necessity are perceived as threatening and inviting the human experiment, though many go on as if business-as-usual still in fact hangs together and makes sense.

What this says is that *there is not so much a generation gap today as a world-view gap.* Two ways of putting life together, of trying to make sense out of things, vie for the future of man—or put more precisely, vie over whether man is to have a future. It is no accident, therefore, that the central theme in

the speeches and writings of the Berrigan brothers
is the struggle of life against death.

THE STATE IN THE STRUGGLE
OF LIFE AGAINST DEATH

There are two traditional sources for the authority
of government. One is its promise to preserve and
ameliorate the conditions of human life. The other
is its monopoly of "legitimate" death and the ability
to exercise this power effectively against internal
and external opposition. The first and more positive
of these sources is in fact preeminent. For government, if it is to be successful for any length of time,
depends upon majority consent. To be sure, consent
can be coerced or subverted, but only at a high
price in terms of implicit social stability and
strength. "You can do anything with bayonets except sit on them." Our own Declaration of Independence recognized this priority of the promise to
serve life over the threat of dealing death when it
placed life as the first of the inalienable human
rights which, if denied, constituted justification for
revolution.

However, this priority of life over death has remained up to now politically unfocused and mostly
inoperative. The reason for this is that the traditional practical conditions and consciousness of man
permitted the peculiar luxury of viewing life as
if its first order of business were about something
else besides living. Indeed, this is the essential nature of what we may call the *old state* which viewed
and constructed itself as a public arena for com-
peting vitalities, for the successful pursuit of private
advantage and gain. The polity of the old state, ir-
respective of particulars as regards economic and

political organization, centered upon the consolidation of this sphere of private advantage. It did this through the development of a favorable political and legal intrastructure and through the production of an anger-deflecting scheme of higher justifications, which rendered the given system of social control and benefit an aura of necessity as reflecting the very nature of reality itself.

This is how the established system "made sense" of itself, setting up internalized controls against any emigration from its given universe of reality, which could then be understood simply therapeutically as forms of mental illness (see R.D. Laing on schizophrenia). Conversely, an established system of governance that is no longer able to "make sense of itself" is in fundamental crisis precisely because it can no longer control the definitions of that reality within which it is located. Consequently, *significant* internal emigrations begin to fracture its social massiveness, solidity and persuasiveness.

Clearly, not only we in America but almost all advanced industrial nations currently find themselves in the midst of such a crisis. Various theses have been advanced to explain this remarkable coincidence: theses dealing with technology, with rational/bureaucratic values, with affluence and released repressions, and so on. However our argument here points us to another (supplementary?) root. Namely, there is a rise of the new consciousness which sees mankind as having outgrown the old luxury of simply assuming his continuing existence, a consciousness which has come to perceive the promise of life as man's own responsibility and task. Under these conditions, what we have called the old state passes into a fundamental crisis of authority as it is forced to face what it had hitherto been able to take for granted and so ignore—that is, the struggle between life and death which lies at the foundations of all authority and government among men. The declaration of the inalienable right to life set forth in the Declaration of Independence, unlike its original setting where the political dynamics involved simply the transfer of elites, now becomes a genuinely revolutionary idea and mandate.

COMING HOME TO THE HOMELAND EARTH

As the new consciousness struggles with this revolutionary demand of life against death, it is pushed to define a new and fundamentally different human project of life. This can be summarized in terms of a new necessity, that *man must come home if he is to have a home.* There is an urgent sense that the world is first of all man's homeland—not a battlefield, or tally sheet, or factory, or commodity supermarket—and that man must come home to this home if he is to have one much longer. This life project implies, in turn, a new life style founded upon a new definition of man's relationship to his social and cultural environment. For if man is to come home to the world as his own home, then man must also *come home to himself and his own project and task.* If his activity is to become first of all home-making activity, then man must actively take hold of his activity in the world as his own activity and responsibility, in order to redirect himself to the priorities of life.

Thus, it begins to appear to him that he can no longer afford to live self-forgetfully, passing the weight of his life off his own hands to become a passive extension of his tools, a product of his products. This is the source of the anti-Madison Avenue life styles of the new culture peoples. For they find there a manipulation which is not so much external but internal, a perversion of the very definition of self, of meaningful and valuable existence, of the direction and success of life. And they perceive in this precisely that age-old reversal which man can no longer afford—man's production of himself to serve the needs and prerequisites of his own creations, his surrender and loss of himself in his products.

Behind this cultural inversion is that old luxury of a world and future taken for granted that permits man's gaze to be deflected from noticing himself as the responsible agent of his own creation and preservation: the producer of all his products, the definer of all his definitions, the valuer of all his valuings. Thus, where the Bowery Bank advertises for depositors under the title "The Good Life" (*New York Times*, June 10, 1970) and proceeds to identify that life with "the beautiful people" playing on a summer beach and "getting away from it all," the new consciousness perceives instead the followers of death who turn aside from life under the illusion that there is in fact some place left to "get away from it all."

What we see in the new consciousness, then, is a kind of spasm reflex of the species gazing in horror upon its own possible extinction. For as man seeks to come home to himself as his own task and creation and so come home to the world as the homeland of his own experiment, he finds himself in a kind of Alice in Wonderland world where nothing is as it appears to be: where hollowmen merchants hawk their superfluities (after careful motivational

research) under the banners of what "free-think-
ing" young men and "liberated" women buy, wear,
and bare; where politicians pontificate about the
proper pursuit of peace being the prudent pursuit
of war; and where authorities insist upon honored
recognition of their power while the whole is out
of control. The new consciousness sees a call for
law and order that decries violence nevertheless
imposes massive violence upon the poor and black
and vocally dissenting at home and peasant "enemies" abroad. It finds the established ego ideals
full of petty virtues and major vices, confusing man-
ners with morality, self-confident piety with holy
dread.

At the same time, the old way of handling this
vision of evil and hypocrisy—the old realism which
could afford to convert the fact into an artifact and
so transform the perception of human suffering and
injustice into a mere sensibility, into a profound
reflection—is a psychic luxury that the new consciousness knows it can no longer afford. It has no
way of transmuting this vision of the world running
over a cliff, the horrifying absurdity of it, into a
mere tragic sense of life. The old exorcisms no
longer work. For we know ourselves now, not as
ironic spectators unfolding distances between ourselves and life's drama, but as active participants
in the destruction of the future.

Under these conditions, man's coming home to
his homeland earth leads to a burning wound of the
spirit that knows no way to heal itself, except perhaps to leap in the path of the absurdity. This must
appear to those of the old world as an outburst of
medieval self-mortification or, in some cases, even
of a drive toward self-destruction. It is, in fact, the

opposite: the desperate attempt to turn mankind's headlong rush toward death to life.

THE BERRIGANS AND THE FOLLOWERS OF LIFE

In his intriguing book *Life Against Death*, Norman O. Brown draws attention to the fact that the contemporary church has lost its capacity to exorcise demons. This is evidence, Brown claims, that at a deeper level formal religion in the West has lost its original power of being, its power of nurturing, healing, and so of preserving human life. This has rendered men of sensitivity peculiarly exposed and floundering in face of the crisis of paralysis at the spiritual depth of modern society. For he has precious little to defend himself from the evil spirits of meaninglessness, absurdity and death he must wrestle with there. He is left wounded upon the field, as has always been the case, but now without a physician of the soul.

This insight locates quite precisely, I believe, the relationship between the Berrigan brothers and the new consciousness peoples. For the activity of the Berrigans is best understood as fundamentally *priestly activity*. They are attempting to regain an ancient heritage and power: to become practitioners of the healing of souls. They have sensed the demons at loose in the spiritual depths of modern man and society—the onslaught of absurdity and death. And they have undertaken to recapture the original priestly task and calling—the struggle of exorcism and liberation. Moreover, they have understood and accepted the traditional price that is demanded of those who would place themselves in the path of the powers of the demonic, of the great

Destroying: with inevitably inadequate and failing weapons, to invoke a rebirth of the power of life over death in a time when the spirit may not respond but only disappoint.

To be sure, to many this may sound excessively "supernatural," a return perhaps to the ghostly anachronisms of "medieval priest-talk." Let that be. Those who have looked into the eyes of the Vietnamese peasant and seen there the horror and incomprehension; those who have entered, even a little, into the life stories of a Malcolm X or Angela Davis or the black boy in the aching apartment house next door; those who have been asked those quiet, overwhelming classroom questions by our most sensitive and intelligent and have had no way to answer; those who have been grasped by the vision of just another silent solar system which, for a while, was magnificently adorned with the voices of a bright blue agate; all those who have seen the destruction of the innocent —these, I think, will understand.

For they understand what's happening in the depths of our time and nation. And they understand, well beyond these words to convey, the unutterably precious task and precarious journey the Berrigans and the followers of life have entered upon. For they are the keepers of mankind's most original and universal faith, without which we would not have arrived at the place where we are, and without which we shall not pass much further beyond.

Gordon C. Zahn

The
Berrigans:
Radical
Activism
Personified

The Catholic peace radicals of my generation
are increasingly troubled by the failure of Catholic
peace radicals of this generation to avoid violence.
We are inclined to be suspicious of what seems
to be a growing willingness to accept violence as
a tactic. Today's Catholic antiwar agitators are
apparently gravitating more and more in the direction of the New Left and forming alliances with
groups like the Black Panthers, condoning if not
actually endorsing the often senselessly disruptive
and destructive acts and rhetoric such groups tend
to promote.

We have, first, the introduction of direct action
tactics which have gone beyond protest to actual
attempts to disrupt the war effort or the operations
of some agency or program related to the war
effort. The series of raids upon offices of draft
boards and prominent manufacturers of war ma-
teriel initiated by Rev. Philip Berrigan, S.S.J.,
and his fellow members of the "Baltimore Four"
on October 27, 1967, and repeated by him and an
expanded group, this time including his Jesuit
brother Daniel (The "Catonsville Nine") on May
17, 1968, marked a dramatic new turn in radical

peace action. Furthermore, as the raids proliferated throughout the country—in Milwaukee, Chicago, San Francisco, New York, Washington, D.C. (against Dow Chemical instead of the Selective Service System), Indianapolis, Minneapolis-St. Paul, Boston—it became evident that this was an almost exclusively Catholic operation.

It would be a mistake to measure the impact of these raids only in terms of repeat performance ratios, the increasing numbers of persons involved, and the extent to which they succeeded in destroying draft files. Of at least equal importance were the "festivals" of support which drew admirers and well-wishers from all over the country as the various cases came to trial. Through these mass celebrations, and the hundreds of smaller gatherings organized to meet and talk with the "criminals" while the legal proceedings against them lumbered along, it is a conservative estimate to say that tens of thousands were reached by the action and many of these were undoubtedly moved to more direct opposition to the war.

In the face of such exciting evidence of success, it is difficult to criticize the Berrigan raids. The difficulty is greatly magnified in my own case by the fact that some of my past writings have been cited in several of the trials as factors in the decision to turn to this new level of radical peace activity. At the same time it would be less than honest to ignore the fact that strongly dissenting views have been expressed within what is usually described as the peace movement and, though I certainly do not share the more condemnatory of these judgments, I do share some of their underlying misgivings. Since these misgivings reflect the differences between the two generations of peace radicals, it is perhaps in order to discuss them briefly.

One thing must be made perfectly clear, however. In no sense are these comments to be taken as an "attack" upon the Berrigans or the others who have followed their inspiring leadership. I count them and several of their followers among my most valued personal friends, and even were this not the case, I would regard them and their commitment with awe and admiration. I have been shocked and offended by the insensitive criticisms and thoroughly unjustified condemnations directed against them by so many Catholics, including fellow priests and bishops, who seem to have a far greater capacity for indignation over the napalming of draft files than they have been able to muster over the napalming of Vietnamese civilians.

As moral witness, I would challenge the right of anyone to fault the acts of these courageous men and women, lay and religious. In the sanctuary of their individual consciences they concluded that the traditional forms of opposition to the war no longer held promise of success, that only some dramatic act of resistance and obstruction could have any impact at all upon a continuing moral evil. Once convinced of this, they decided for themselves that the prison witness has now become the only appropriate witness for the Christian who wishes to dissociate himself completely from an unjust and immoral war and the deep-seated social injustices that war is designed to perpetuate. So they acted—as, indeed, any Christian who reaches such moral convictions would be obliged to act.

This is not to say that their analysis of the situation must be accepted by everyone without question. Those of us who have not yet seen fit to join them generally do not agree that all other forms of protest and opposition have run their course. If we continue to speak and march and sign petitions, this is not to be taken as a *prima facie* confession of moral cowardice (though, in all honesty, we cannot exclude that possibility); instead it is to be read as an affirmation, possibly overly optimistic, that something can still be accomplished within and through "the system" they have rejected.

Time may well prove the Berrigans are absolutely right. It has become far more difficult to defend the potency of conventional forms of protest when we consider a President unwilling to stir from his televised football game to note the presence of a half-million American citizens marching outside to protest his policies. Add to this display of callous indifference the incredibly stupid statements periodically issued by the Vice-President and other highly placed officials, and the suggestion that democratic processes have reached a final and dead end takes on new validity. When an Agnew attacks the news media, how far are we from a Goebbels? When a Julius Hoffman displays a level of judicial temperament and decorum that would have won the admiration of Roland Freisler and his *Volksgericht,* is it really enough to send off a new flurry of telegrams to Congressmen and Senators?

However one may answer these troubling questions, it is clear (or should be) that the Berrigan-style peace activism presents no problem *as personal witness* and, as such, deserves the respect and the support of every committed Christian. My own problem with it is at the level of *communication*, the level at which all the differences discussed earlier become relevant to the issue. In all fairness I must add that some of the participants in these raids with whom I have discussed my misgivings object to the distinction itself, insisting that the action must be judged only as witness. Were this actually the case, however, there would have been little point in making all the elaborate arrangements to have the press—and, if possible, television cameras as well—on the scene to record the "crime."

It is clear, too, that the very symbols employed— the pouring of blood at Baltimore, the use of home-made napalm at Catonsville and in the subsequent raids—testify to an overriding intent to make a point, to get a message across as effectively as possible. This, I submit, is communication and to that extent it can be judged as communication. And the first judgment to be made is that as communication it was astonishingly successful. The hundreds of supporters who rallied to the defendants' support, who traveled great distances to join the trial "celebrations" heard, understood, and accepted that message. Some of them accepted it to the point of going forth to do likewise.

If this were the whole story, the operation would have to be voted a complete success. Unfortunately, there is more to be taken into account. It is evident that tremendous numbers of people, including as already noted many already engaged in peace activities, were "turned off" by what seemed to them an altogether excessive form of protest. Certainly these included those who were already committed to support for the war effort and who were only too ready to take this as one more evidence of the unreasonableness of any dissent in wartime.

Much more serious a negative effect, however, was the amount of adverse reaction on the part of others who had been hitherto uncommitted. As a native Milwaukeean with continuing ties to that community I can testify to the strength of the opposition to the "Milwaukee Fourteen" raid, including I might add, expressions of indignant disapproval by individuals who had provided me with support and encouragement during the full period of my service as a conscientious objector to World War II.

The only real test of the raids as communication—whether more of the uncommitted were turned off or won over—is beyond our power to determine at this time. If, as I would guess, the balance was negative, they were at least a partial failure. That some lukewarm opponents of the war were fired up to the point that they assumed a more direct and active role is an argument in the Berrigans' favor; however, this too would have to be measured against others who may have been pushed or scared away.

One final point has to be made in this connection. In weighing the relative importance of the dimensions of witness and communication, the former must be given unquestioned priority. One must always act as his conscience demands, even at the price of alienating others. A hypothetical parallel might be helpful here. Had a similar group of Catholic priests and laymen invaded some offices in Nazi Germany to remove, deface, and destroy the lists of Jews scheduled for deportation to the extermination camps, few of us would be inclined to criticize them today for their "extremism." And this would hold true even if it could be shown that the majority of the "good" Germans of the time did not understand or were offended by their action. Here, too, one cannot be sure of just how "hypothetical" this parallel may be; time and added perspective may show that this is where the Berrigans and their fellow criminals are and where the rest of us should be.

One part of the Berrigan message did come through loud and clear to both the opponents and the supporters of their action. Whether so intended or not, the draft board raids contributed, on the one hand, to the new mood of radical dissent which takes it for granted that one is free to disregard and disobey any law with which he does not agree—and, on the other, to the conviction held by Mr. Nixon's "silent majority" that dissent as such is an invitation to anarchy. Both positions, it should be noted, represent a distorted understanding of a perfectly valid principle of civil disobedience, namely that an immoral or unjust law is no law and not only may be, but should be, disobeyed.

The crucial difference between this formulation and that which is in the ascendancy today is that "classic" civil disobedience is specific: the offensive law or practice, or even authority, is identified and the faults are spelled out as part of the act of disobedience itself. Increasingly this standard is being abandoned in favor of highly indiscriminate and individualized rejection of all authority which is then justified in the name of a vaguely defined and romanticized revolutionary ideal. What finally results in all too many instances is a frankly unprincipled exploitation of any or every issue or grievance in the interest of creating as much civil disruption as possible.

The resulting "polarization" is then interpreted as a value in its own right and as a means for promoting further revolutionary progress. Underlying this rationale is the highly dubious assumption that a final and forced choice between revolutionaries and reactionaries will result in the victory of the former. History would seem to argue instead that in any such ultimate confrontation, the Right, rather than right, is more likely to win out. The much-scorned liberal is frequently chided for his commitment to the illusion that it is still possible to use normal political processes to gain his socially desirable ends; it would seem a far more dangerous illusion that a few strident slogans and random destructive outbursts will bring "the System" to a point of collapse. What these are far more likely to accomplish is to convert subtle repression into overt repression and with the approval, or at least the silent acquiescence, of the dominant majority.

One need not deny that this nation may have reached a critical point in its history where revolution, in the sense of a total and rapid restructuring of the social order, is the only way by which it can free itself for its own and the world's good from the chains of war, militarism, racism, and economic imperialism. But if this is the situation, as I am prepared to say it is, it will require much more than the extravagant rhetoric and self-righteous posturings that pass for a revolutionary stance in some of our more activist circles. I do not, be it noted, include the Berrigans and their raids under this description. On the contrary,

they could serve as models of carefully calculated
and disciplined civil disobedience. I do suggest,
however, that the dramatic quality of the raids,
together with the sometimes excessive emotional
reactions they provoked on the part of many of
the young admirers who trooped to the trial celebrations, contributed to the spread of the "anything
goes, anytime" mood that is so widespread among
many of the younger elements of the peace—or, to
be more accurate, antiwar—movement.

The latter distinction in terms is crucial as the
two massive demonstrations held on Boston Common in October 1969 and April 1970 revealed. On
the surface they seemed quite similar. The October
turnout of a hundred thousand people or so was
almost matched by the April rally. Both represented a broad coalition of individuals and groups
opposing the war in Vietnam. But here the simi-
larity breaks down. October's was a gloriously
happy affair; the crowd's enthusiasm was evi-
denced in the waves of applause that greeted each
speaker and punctuated his remarks; and the
speakers themselves reveled in their common purpose, playing down or avoiding altogether the
ideological and tactical points of difference that
separated them and their organizations.

April was something else. The tone of the
gathering was sullen, even bitter, as it was exposed
to a seemingly endless parade of speakers who were
intensely particularistic in their various separate
appeals. In place of the surges of spontaneous and
enthusiastic response, each speaker was greeted
with scattered applause from those segments of the
crowd already in his camp while the great majority
listened in silence or ignored him altogether. As for
the speeches themselves, they seemed designed to

affront those listeners who were not already part of the speaker's following. Rational argumentation was replaced in many instances by reliance upon the rather limited stock of sex-related expletives and ritual clichés. Cue words ("pig") and slogans ("Right on!," "Power to the people!") were *de rigueur* for any speaker who wanted his full share of the scattered applause.

Perhaps the most depressing note of the whole affair was the frequency with which the representatives of one group would be openly scornful of the objectives of another; indeed, the advocates of pacifism and nonviolence were ridiculed and repudiated, one speaker using his time to call upon the thousands ostensibly gathered there to express their desire for peace to "pick up the gun." Only at the very end of the rally when the local "tribe" of *Hair* called upon the world to "let the sun shine in" did the crowd show any sign of catching fire, but by then it was too late. Most had already drifted away, bored or offended by the speakers or, in the case of a sizeable segment, on their way to the night of destructive rioting and "trashing" in Harvard Square that followed.

The difference between the two events reflects a change in mood that has its expression in the substitution of the symbol of the clenched red fist for that of the dove and the olive branch. It is easy enough to understand the reason; the October rally, for all its success as an event, had been singularly unsuccessful in affecting national policy and the great outpouring of people for the November rally in Washington had been studiously ignored. The war and its casualties continued; domestic needs grew more pressing while the nation's resources were being squandered on the battlefields of Southeast Asia.

But to understand does not necessarily mean to accept the new emphasis, and this is where the old-line pacifists, the peace radicals of yesterday, have been forced to question the wisdom and the usefulness of actions and rhetoric which introduce and exploit new animosities in the interests of what appears to be an intensified commitment to violence and destruction. They find it ever more difficult to distinguish the slogans of the New Left ("We want peace, and we will use any means to get it!") from those of the ultra-hawks as they call for the total destruction of those they define as enemy. They fear, and with good reason, that the tiger their young associates have chosen to ride is not heading down the paths of peace and fellowship among all men.

As the center of peace activism continues to move more and more in the direction of aggressive, even disruptive and destructive, activism, the prospects for further fragmentation within the peace movement become more certain. Directed and disciplined civil disobedience will have less appeal as the logic of events takes hold. Once again it is helpful to turn to the draft-board raids to illustrate the point. Probably the most compelling rationale for these raids was that given to one of my classes at the university by Tony Mullaney, the Benedictine priest member of the "Milwaukee Fourteen." As he explained it, every Christian has an obligation to be what he called "a public speaker" in the sense of dedicating his life and his acts to the spread of the Christian message and to work for the removal of social evil and injustice. To this end, he had "gone the route" and tried everything:

he had marched and he had preached; he had signed petitions and written letters; he had picketed and participated in mass demonstrations—and all to no avail. No one, he was forced to conclude, was listening; or, if leaders heard, they did not heed. In order to make his point, to be the "public speaker" he had to be, it became necessary, he felt, to "raise the ante." For him that meant journeying to Milwaukee, invading the draft office there, and destroying as many of its records as he could.

It is an extremely persuasive case, at least until we raise the next question: what if *that* doesn't work? And obviously it has not worked; both the war and the draft go on. Though it is possible to argue that the raised ante may have contributed to decisions to reform the draft and the proposals to abandon it altogether—and even, I suppose, to the decision to begin removing men from Vietnam—it would be difficult to establish that this was a major factor. On the other hand, there are those who would insist—and with at least as much logic—that the draft board raids can be shown to have lost their original impact so that now they can be shrugged off as little more than inconsequential nuisances.

If so, what must the next step be? Does one move on to bombing the offices themselves, first with advance warning and then, if the war still goes on, without the warning? To my knowledge these hypothetical next steps in the sequence have not been proposed by anyone involved in or sympathetic toward the Berrigan raids. Nevertheless, I would not be at all sure that there are not some peace radicals around who might be prepared to give such proposals their assent.

Which is only to say, in effect, that even the Berrigans may be in danger of slipping into my "sometime radical" category. In fact, they may already be there. Thus, for instance, criticism has been voiced against the practice of waiting to be arrested after the "criminal" act is performed. As the "hit-and-run and be ready to hit-and-run again" mode of operation gains favor, it is entirely possible that the burners of draft files, like the burners of draft cards before them, may find their actions rejected as examples of ego-serving, bourgeois tokenism.

There is some evidence that the Catonsville raiders are themselves split on this issue. The decision of four of them to "go underground" as fugitives after their Supreme Court appeal was denied should not be read as an attempt to evade the personal unpleasantness of spending several years in prison. Instead, the decision represents something of an ideological shift. In Dan Berrigan's words, the purpose is to "show them they can no longer lock people up on their order, any more than they can induct people into the military service on their order." This is, of course, a perfectly acceptable rationale, and one is free to hope (as I do) that the fugitives succeed in evading capture so that they may continue to work against the war. This does not alter the very significant fact, however, that it is quite a different rationale from the one originally set forth.

In the early raids, the governing rationale centered upon the principles of Christian non-violent resistance *including* the crucial spiritual dimension of accepting the penalty *because of the*

continued witness the penalty itself represents. It is
my recollection that some members of the Catonsville Nine, Dan Berrigan among them, were ambiv-
alent about putting up any court defense at all
lest the clarity of their witness be confused and
lost. Needless to say, it is not for the "guilty
bystander" who would not be called upon to serve
the sentence in any case, to decide which of the
two formulations is the better or in which form the
witness is more effective. It is the shift itself that
interests me and the fact that it has been in the
direction of what is generally taken to be a more
radical stance.

Whether it actually is more radical or not is
the final question to be raised and discussed. How
one answers the question will determine who is
entitled to the peace radical designation. Returning
to the personal framework I have employed here, I
have not destroyed draft records or, for that
matter, draft cards (though I have violated the law
by accepting draft cards that were turned in at a
Resistance rally). Nor have I encouraged others to
do so; in fact, I have argued against the draft-board
raids with friends who were subsequently involved
in this kind of action. If one measures radicalism
by the dramatic content of an act and the degree
of illegality involved, I am not (nor, I fear have I
ever been) much of a radical.

If, on the other hand, we take the term to
mean a firm conviction based on an informed
interpretation of fundamental moral principle and
a pattern of behavior which gives expression to
that conviction, all is not lost. By this standard, the
conscientious objector performing his alternate
service is as much a "radical" as the federal
prisoner whose conscience told him that this was

not enough. Of course, the C.O. who does recognize a moral obligation to violate the law but accepts alternate service instead could not be so designated, though his witness should not be written off completely. By the same token, the individual who is not personally convinced that it is right and necessary to violate the law but feels impelled to follow the raucous crowd which tells him that "this is where it's at," or who is swept into his activism by the appeal of greater drama and risk, should not be classified too readily as a radical either. The radicalism, in short, lies in the moral commitment, not in the manifestation alone.

If this seems a rather inconclusive note on which to end this discussion, it is nonetheless crucial. Conformism can come in many shades and forms, and a truly radical activity is more than a matter of ego-gratification through exhibitionistic extravagance. The elements of Catholic peace radicalism, as I see them, must include the following: first and most essential, a thoroughgoing commitment to the Gospel message of peace and love; second, a conviction that the Christian must always be prepared to act according to that commitment and as his conscience instructs, regardless of the consequences he may have to suffer; third, he must do so in a spirit of charity toward those not yet aware of the pacifist implications of their faith; and, finally, he must so govern his behavior that nothing he may do will violate or contradict those principles he has set out to serve.

Some may feel that such a formulation is too "open," that it includes too wide a range of individual witnesses under the rubric of radicalism. Nevertheless, to the extent that it insists upon the primacy of the individual conscience and incorporates fundamental Christian ideals of all-inclusive and self-sacrificing love, it is radical in the fullest and truest sense of the word. Which is only to suggest that the Cross and neither the olive branch nor the fist still holds promise of being the most radical symbol of all.

This formulation I have offered allows all the room in the world for the courage and the creativity of the Berrigans and the other new-breed radicals who, quite rightly, have taken over the leadership of the Catholic peace movement; but it does so without denying or rejecting the witness of my generation of peace radicals—or, for that matter, of men like Franziskus Stratmann of Germany and Paul Hanly Furfey and others in America who provided us with so great a measure of inspiration and support.

If, as I for one am ready and happy to acknowledge, today's radicals are more likely to succeed in finally "turning the Church around" and bringing it back to full awareness of what was its original pacifist mission, it is perhaps important that we not overlook altogether the sometime radicals who brought them to their starting point. In this sense still, if in no other, it does all go together.

Rosemary Radford Ruether

Beyond Confrontation: The Therapeutic Task

The question which has been taxing my mind for some time is this: how do we go beyond scenarios of outrage and moral disaffiliation from the evils of our times and find modest but real ways to transform the situation? I am not sure that this has to do with creating a "new man," that moral eschatology held out to us so alluringly by the Berrigans, Castro, and St. Paul. I suspect it has to do precisely with some insufficient and ambiguous tinkering with "outward circumstances" which make life a little more livable for a few more people. As one recent writer put it:

> Revolutions and revolutionaries become terrifying when they go beyond mere change of "outer" circumstances and institutions and speak of a "new man" shorn and cleansed of racism, inferiority feelings, bourgeois values, etc. A "new man" is a logical and historical impossibility. The logical impossibility lies in the fact that the new man is either a somewhat changed man, though with a memory and hence not new; or else he is so "new" that he no longer remembers what he was and did, and thus is no longer a man.

The essence of neurosis and unhappiness is the denial of the past and the refusal to come to terms with it. The preconditions for mass control are the eradication of personal and collective pasts. Black people know this in a way that white people do not. They know what it is to be denied a past. White Americans would like to deny their past by glossing over it with myths of American innocence or else by seeing it as stained beyond redemption. To go beyond our past, however, we must not deny it; rather we must understand it and thereby work through it.
(Richard King, "Thoughts on Race and Radicalism," *D.C. Gazette*, Vol. II, No. 4, Feb. 1–14, 1971, p. 7)

This is not a question about which I feel any particular need to coax out some strained and far-fetched criticism of the Berrigans either. I think they have done just about perfectly the thing they set about to do. They have seen the madness and have shown us how the individual person stands against it, without compromise but also concretely, existentially, and not just rhetorically. Their witness has a completeness and clarity that fills the heavens with its rightness and before which one can only say "Amen," and even "right on."

But that witness, although complete and perfect in terms of the particular question and answer with which it concerns itself, is also necessarily limited in scope. For some time I have been trying to answer for myself this other question, which does not lend itself to this kind of clarity of witness and on which the Berrigans shed no light whatsoever. This is not their fault. Nobody can do everything, and when someone does his thing as well as they have done theirs, one has no right to complain. But the fact is that "their thing" does seem to leave some other universes untouched, while suggesting that their own moral universe is the only authentic one, all other considerations being but weak-kneed compromises. Part of the difficulty that one feels right away when one tries to "yes-but" with the Berrigans, is that their style is designed to produce great gobs of self-sickening guilt in the beholder. One is meant to be left with no alternative but humble discipleship or else mean-spirited maliciousness. There isn't supposed to be any ground left from which one can say: "Well, okay, but how about this other thing?" And within a certain framework I think that either/or is legitimate. Nevertheless I feel compelled to go on to something else, which has made that Berrigan moral universe somewhat less than compelling to me at the moment. The fact of the matter is that I groove too easily on the Berrigans' thing and that is why I have become uncomfortably aware of its limitations. There is a certain sort of moral outrage—confrontation with powers and principalities of the evil world, stance of uncompromising rejection and rejoicing over the fall of Babylon—for which I have an uncommon natural skill. I do that sort of thing well. I have written a lot of speeches in that style, and I have stood behind various barricades and told off various wielders of evil power, in prophetic rhetoric that bloomed a thing of beauty. And I am not mocking: they *were* things of beauty, and I will stand by them for what they are worth. I know very well that mood of exaltation in which one could bash a draft office, make a fine court-room speech and become that sort of outlaw which clearly witnesses to our need to separate ourselves unequivocably from this corrupt society. And that is very good. Yet I find myself nagged by this other question that opens up a different moral universe, and none of this excellent moral outrage really helps me with this other question at all.

Allow me an example. A short while ago some people from Women's Strike for Peace asked me to lead a delegation to the Justice Department to confront the leaders there with the total outrage of their recent (fabricated) indictment against Philip Berrigan and twelve other defendants and "co-conspirators." Some of the women were a little timid to expose themselves in this foray. Others felt they might be inarticulate. They wanted a strong spokesman, and I was asked to be that sort of spokesman. The scene at the Justice Department was nothing short of Kafkaesque. Our little delegation of middle-class ladies was treated by the Justice Department as so many incipient Weather-mothers. We were surrounded by security personnel immediately upon our arrival. A storm trooper with gloves and a large gun took our identification. We were covertly photographed, and lied to when we protested. An agent escorted us in a separate elevator to an upper room. There we were surrounded by watchful agents. The room was obviously bugged, and I suspect had a hidden camera as well to record our visit in detail. After a period of isolation presumably designed to induce traumas of intimidation, one Francis Xavier Worthington, Chief of the Internal Security Division of the Justice Department, with aides, swept into the room, and coolly inquired as to our business. Rising to the occasion I had at the good man in fine and incisive style. All of his tricks and foils I laid bare and discarded. Having taken apart every piece of his armor to our complete satisfaction, we rose and marched from the room. The ladies were lavish with heart-felt congratulations: "You were magificent, Rosemary." With new heart, they contacted an A.C.L.U. lawyer and some news-papermen, and the whole style of the Justice Department was duly laid bare in the *Washington Post*. The article was crowned by a final devastating remark by myself about the "fascist, paranoid atmosphere of super-security that characterizes the Justice Department."

I am very glad I did that. I may also say that I enjoyed the occasion greatly, because, as I mentioned before, I have a certain talent for confrontation. But I am not satisfied.

We gave some more fuel to those who already agree with us, and that is not a bad thing to do. But we did nothing whatsoever to relieve that fascist paranoia of the Justice Department. On the contrary, we probably heightened it, and perhaps made it a bit more skillful in concealing itself next time. After all, those people are not stupid. The sort of thing we did was fine, within its limits, but I would really have liked to do something else; something I am not very good at doing; indeed something I scarcely know how to begin going about: something which seems to me to be the real "nonviolent" task, far more important than the scenarios of moral outrage and disaffiliation. I would really like to have gotten under Mr. Francis Xavier Worthington's skin and, in some way that didn't throw him on the defensive at all, tricked him into discovering for himself that all this was unnecessary. All this security, all this counterattack upon the cries that well up from the streets; all this elaborate work of defense is really unnecessary. It is not what he wants. It is not what he needs. It doesn't really follow from his real ideals and concerns for his country. You see, I think we must start with the understanding that Mr. Francis Xavier Worthington does have ideals and concerns, and that is why he acts in the way that he does. After every one of his manipulations has been exposed, when Mr. Worthington finally draws himself erect and says to us "Well, this is still the best country in the world," we should stifle our impulse to whistle in amazement and despair, for he is really not being a hypocrite! He is desperately trying to hold on to the straw of that faith in which he believes and to which he has dedicated the best years of his life, these last fifteen years in the Internal Security Division of the Justice Department. If we don't understand that Mr. Francis Xavier Worthington is a dedicated and idealistic man, just as dedicated and idealistic (according to his lights) as Daniel Berrigan, S.J., and Philip Berrigan, S.S.J., then we will never understand anything at all about Mr. Francis Xavier Worthington, and especially we will never understand why it has become terribly important to him that Daniel and Philip Berrigan be smeared, discredited, and cast into outer darkness. The point is that Daniel and Philip Berrigan have met Mr. Worthington on his own ground; Good American and Good, Jesuit-trained Catholic that he is, they have laid upon him the terrible and truthful judgment which he cannot possibly bear to accept, and for that reason they have become far more "dangerous" to Mr. Worthington's internal security than all the pushers on fourteenth street.

Subjectively Mr. Francis Xavier Worthington is a good man. Objectively, he is probably doing about

as much evil as anyone in the world. Shall we
strip him naked, and show him the the corpses
of destroyed lives that are strewn at his feet?
Or is there a place even here for anger to be
checked by sympathy, notwithstanding the fact
that, as yet, he has learned nothing. I would like
to ask God to please do us a little favor and pluck
this demon from the back of Mr. Francis Xavier
Worthington. Allow him to wake up one morning
with the sudden amazing discovery that he can
be rid of it. I don't even want to have to confront
him with it. I don't think his psychic structure can
bear the bad news of the total moral failure
of his life, if that means having to live with the
image of the righteous ones of the like of Daniel
and Philip Berrigan before his eyes. I think that
if he could just sort of slough it all off one fine
morning, we could perhaps conspire to help him
save face in respect to those priests whom he is
presently trying to crucify. Poor Mr. Worthington
does need to believe that he is a good man after
all; good father, loyal American, faithful member
of the Knights of Columbus that he has always
been. I wouldn't want to take all that away from
him.

So it is this that dims the clarity of my moral
righteousness and is the reason why I can take no
delight in the excellent rhetoric finely hewn in
blood by those best of prophets, Daniel and Philip
Berrigan. And it not only clouds my satisfaction
with the confronting of Mr. Francis Xavier Worthington—it steals a bit of the thrust from my
confrontation with the whole damn country. When
I pick up my phone and hear that peculiar echoing
sound that indicates that the F.B.I. has it on an
"open line," I can't get up a satisfying fund

of outrage. I feel sad, and most of all I feel sympathetic fellow-feeling with all those righteous and
high-minded men who busy themselves defaming
and destroying their fellow citizens and prolonging
the agony of helpless people around the world.
I would like to reach out and pat that diligent spy
gently on the head and say, "That's all right, honey.
I've got good news for you. The war is over."

Philip Nobile

Phil
Berrigan
in
Prison

Father Philip Berrigan refused to give himself
up to federal marshals on April 9, 1970, the day
he was to begin serving a six-year sentence for
his share in the Baltimore Four and Catonsville
Nine draft-board actions. Together with Philip
Berrigan in this one last measure of resistance
were accomplices David Eberhardt, George Mische,
Mary Moylan, and his Jesuit brother, Daniel Berrigan. The strategy of the group was strictly *ad hoc*.
At first, they thought they would remain in hiding
for only a brief interlude and then surrender at
a time and place of their own, not the government's,
choosing. Press releases swiftly rolled off Catholic
underground machines announcing Dan Berrigan's
forthcoming appearance at a Cornell peace rally
April 19 and Philip Berrigan and David Eberhardt's appoinment two nights later at St. Gregory
the Great Church on Manhattan's Upper West
Side. "Federal marshals are expected to haul the
two priests away in chains at these occasions," said
one release dated April 13.

Plans changed, however. Dan Berrigan decided
against submission and slipped away from Cornell
for a four-month fugitive run. George Mische

dropped out of sight entirely until his late May capture in Chicago. Mary Moylan was invisible from the start and is still at large.

Philip Berrigan and David Eberhardt went to keep their scheduled rendezvous. Arriving at St. Gregory's before dawn on April 21, they planned to wait out the day in the sanctuary of the rectory under the F.B.I.'s implicit agreement not to interfere until the evening rally was done. Although it is uncertain whether the two outlaws actually would have doublecrossed the authorities by taking flight after the proceedings, a crude escape route was rehearsed by friends in their company. In any case, the F.B.I. removed temptation from Berrigan and Eberhardt by seizing them in a surprise afternoon raid. Pastor Harry Brown, a large man of Old Testament bearing and new politics taste, wept as the F.B.I. broke down his closet door and pulled Philip Berrigan from his final hiding place. Agent Tom Walsh, the leader of the posse, apologized to his old Fordham classmate for coming early. "I'm only one of the Indians," he said to the disconsolate Brown, who has since resigned his pastorate and quit St. Gregory's Parish.

Berrigan and Eberhardt were taken to Lewisburg Federal Penitentiary, a maximum-security institution located in Eastern Pennsylvania. Although Lewisburg is a "big house" for criminals considered dangerous—the reason for its high walls, gun turrets, sliding steel doors, triple locks, and guarded cell blocks—it also serves as a processing point for political prisoners and other low-risk convicts who pass through on their way to Lewisburg Farm or the nearby Allenwood Camp. The latter are minimum-security arrangements, that is, prisons without walls.

The crucial difference between maximum and minimum security, however, is less architectural than psychological. The potential for violence at Lewisburg, where murders, rapes, and beatings among inmates are not uncommon, makes it a scary place to live, especially for peaceful political prisoners who are usually resented by both the general population and the prison staff. In his book *In the Service of Their Country: War Resisters in Prison,* Dr. Willard Gaylin, a Columbia psychiatrist, mentions one Lewisburg incident in which a pacifist prisoner was gang-raped by some fifteen convicts. The event was subsequently covered up in the prison records.

Lewisburg's maximum security is also employed as punishment for political prisoners who get "out of line" in minimum security. Gaylin quotes Mike, a former prisoner at "Oakdale," the name for Lewisburg in his book, on this practice:

> The warden thinks a guy's a wise guy, he'll place him in the general population where the word gets around that he refused to go in service. The hillbillies will do anything to him if they get a chance. They figure if the guy gets a couple of knocks, possibly rape, it'll draw him in line.
> Also at Oakdale there's that big, high wall and that has an impact on anybody who's never been in before. I think the officers are different there too. Once, when I was there I talked with Dr. B., the psychiatrist, who had told the warden about one boy who was sure to get into trouble. The warden said that if he takes a few slaps it'll straighten him out.
> You've got to remember these are very young guys, in addition to looking soft. The hacks call these guys communists and, while I don't

think they would knowingly allow them to get
sexually abused, they will let them take a
punch in the mouth if necessary.'

The horrors of Lewisburg should not have concerned Berrigan and Eberhardt directly. Normally,
they would have been transferred to either Lewisburg Farm or Allenwood Camp in a matter of
days. But May and June went by and both re-
maind captives of Lewisburg's maximum security.

On July 6, after two months of varying degrees
of harrassment, Berrigan and Eberhardt elected
solitary confinement to protest their relatively cruel
and quite unusual punishment. The proximate cause
of this action was a week's suspension of recreation
privileges which both received for two minor
infractions—waiting in the wrong chow line and
being found in an unauthorized part of the prison
(where they went to speak to the chaplain about
Eberhardt's fears of rape). Just before going into
the hole, Berrigan and Eberhardt got detailed
statements out to their Catholic friends. Berrigan
listed eleven examples of harassment and then
went on to explain the politics behind his and
Eberhardt's ordeal:

> The fact is, political prisoners at Lewisburg
> are persecuted beyond the routine dehuman-
> ization given to the other inmates. The rightist
> policies of the staff are proverbial, and they
> profoundly fear anyone standing for justice
> and peace. God, flag, law, order, privilege—
> all mask a policy of falsehood to the men,
> petty persecution, and at worst, brutality of an
> impressive type. Meanwhile official propa-
> ganda boasts of rehabilitation—of tolerance,
> humaneness and creative innovation.

In reality, actual policy toward the men

faithfully repeats the government's duplicity, broken promises and eager resort to naked force. The federal penal system is part of "big government"—one is no better than the other. Prisoners here are largely powerless, colonials not citizens, condemned for their crimes to the "crime of punishment"—from which there is little redress. They get the same essential treatment as blacks and Indochinese.

Personally, I didn't commit civil disobedience twice, submit to three mistrials and accept jail when I could have fled—all to abandon here my sense of justice and humanity. Nor to become suddenly, simply because I am under the power of "re-habilitation experts," a robot and a drone.

Consequently, I reject the punishment given me, refuse work and go to the "hole." There I will begin a fast for the men there, for Vietnamese and Americans in Indochina, for exploited people everywhere—and for their misguided and inhuman oppressors.

After two days in solitary confinement, the equivalent of the original punishment, Berrigan and Eberhardt could have returned to their everyday routine. Instead, they raised the stakes by remaining where they were and starting a fast. On July 9, the second day of this new tactic, Philip Berrigan wrote to Senator Charles Goodell:

Am writing this from a solitary cell in the federal pen here, where I've voluntarily gone to protest the harassment of political prisoners. Before getting into that however, I want to congratulate you on your opposition to the Indochinese war and to say that I hope for your election.
We are of one mind therefore, in a sense—

I'm serving a six year sentence for destruction of draft files. In reference to the harassment —my mail has been tampered with constantly, stool pigeons encouraged to inform on me, guards instructed to report my every move, legitimate visits denied me, guards searching me, my quarters, the sacristy where I vest for Mass. In addition, I have been denied minimum security (one of the farm camps) usually accorded to political prisoners.

The reason alleged for the latter is the fact that we absconded (refusing surrender to U.S. marshals) April 9. (We did abscond to attend a peace rally in NYC, but we did notify both the press and the FBI.) The real reason however is this—my brother, Fr. Daniel Berrigan, is still a fugitive, and everybody thinks that I can help apprehend him. Fortunately, he's wise enough not to let me know where he is.

You may desire to call the Federal Bureau of Prisons, asking them about general treatment of political prisoners, and my treatment specifically, especially the maximum security status in which I'm kept. I'm not a criminal, but a political prisoner, and I have no need for walls, locks and bars.

Also, please contact my lawyer, Harold Buchman (Buchman & Schwartz, Baltimore) about the incongruity of a 6 yr. sentence for burning paper rather than children. Three months ago, a Lt. was sentenced to 6 mos. for killing several civilians in South Vietnam. Others, more clever than he, butcher on a wider scale and get medals. . . .

I have one other point—Congressional doves take it diplomatically easy on the war. A few don't get re-elected; but most sacrifice nothing. (You are a notable exception to this.) Nevertheless, by overall contrast, we have risked our lives repeatedly, and have gone to prison for our convictions. I am in a solitary cell fasting, while my brother is hunted like a killer by the FBI.

I'm indicting no one, I'm merely trying to point out that you need us, as we need you. Without us, you could not perhaps, talk as freely against the war as you do. And without you, there would be complete intransigence from the government.

If there are not people like us on the streets and not in prison, this country may become another Germany. This will be opposed by many people, increasing the likelihood of a national shootout.

I'm suggesting therefore, that you investigate further some of these points. Perhaps you can initiate some real work on amnesty for political prisoners.

Berrigan's letter was about to receive a form reply of concern when Judy Poole, a nineteen-year-old Goodell intern and Cornell SDSer on leave from the barricades, rescued it from the pile and passed it on to Goodell. The Senator reacted most sympathetically. Once a moderately conservative Congressman from upstate New York, Goodell had moved increasingly and consistently left since 1968 when Governor Nelson Rockefeller appointed him to fill Robert Kennedy's unexpired Senate term. He introduced the first end-the-war amendment in September, 1969; he and McGovern were the only Senators to appear at the November, 1969, Moratorium in Washington; he was one of four Senators who voted against military appropriations that December; he introduced a bill to allow for selective conscientious objection and amnesty for draft resisters; he was the first Republican Senator to oppose Judge Carswell's Supreme Court nomination; he also came to the public defense of the Presidio twenty-seven.

Although Goodell had never met his correspondent, he was familiar with the crime and trial of the Catonsville Nine. "I regarded their burning of draft records as an important symbolic act," Goodell said later. "Such acts are necessary when you reach a point of such great frustration that you don't think you can communicate any other way." What brought Goodell to the aid of Philip Berrigan, apart from the maximum security issue, was his feeling that the Catonsville Nine had been denied a fair trial because the judge charged the jury to ignore the good intentions of the defendants. "I believe in a system of law," he said, "but I believe the law was misinterpreted in this case. Constitutional guarantees weren't utilized in the trial itself. The jury should have considered the action of the Catonsville Nine in its proper perspective—the whole backdrop of the war, the lack of responsiveness within the established system and the intent of the individuals. These factors should be relevant to the jury."

Goodell replied to Berrigan July 17.

Thank you very much for your recent letter concerning your confinement at Lewisburg.

Your letter expresses a view which I have always held to be true—this is the view that each man must speak out in his own way. For you, the fight against the machinery of war is not a new one; your actions have shown a profound understanding of the paradoxes and contradictions of our country's position, both moral and political.

Although each man's manner of expression differs, every voice of dissent is essential to the struggle against war, racism and human

suffering. Because individuals such as yourself
have offered an alternative to the killing and
injustices perpetuated in the name of this country, I believe there is reason for hope.

I have personally requested that the Director
of the Federal Bureau of Prisons place you in
minimum security and insure that your personal liberties are protected. I have also contacted your lawyer and several of your friends
regarding the particulars of your case.

At this time, I have directed several members of my staff to begin research for a future
statement concerning political prisoners.

If there is any change in your situation or
any need for assistance, please do not hesitate
to call upon me.

Goodell was carefully low-key in his negotiations
with the Federal Bureau of Prisons. He had no wish
to embarrass the F.B.P. publicly and force them
into a defensive posture from which they would
find it difficult to retreat. Instead of bringing Berrigan's complaint to national attention on the Senate floor, Goodell set in motion a delicate set of
maneuvers that would eventually succeed in gaining the release from maximum security of the three
Catonsville prisoners at Lewisburg—Philip Berrigan, David Eberhardt and George Mische, who
had been brought there after his capture in May.
The Senator took the more traveled bureaucratic
road. And it made all the difference. The first move
was a letter dated July 17, to Dr. Norman A. Carlson, Director of the Federal Bureau of Prisons.
Goodell repeated the charges of harassment and
requested the standard procedure of minimum security for political prisoners be applied to Philip
Berrigan and the other two men. Carlson responded
ten days later.

We received your letter of July 17 concerning Father Philip Berrigan, who is presently confined at the U. S. Penitentiary, Lewisburg, Pennsylvania. Father Berrigan has indicated that he is harassed by the staff of the institution.

Several inquiries have been made regarding similar complaints. As a result, we have looked into Father Berrigan's situation at Lewisburg and are convinced that he has not been harassed.

On July 6 Father Berrigan and a fellow inmate appeared before the adjustment committee on a misconduct charge. They had been found out of bounds and they attempted to enter the waiting line to eat at a time other than scheduled for their group. They were given one week's restriction of privileges, but both refused to accept this restriction. They were instructed to return to their assignments and quarters. Both refused and demanded to be placed in segregation quarters.

Two days later, on July 8, they were to be released from the segregation unit with the understanding that the two-day period of segregation would be the equivalent of the original restrictions imposed. They refused to leave segregation, however, and elected to go on a fast. In keeping with institutional policy, the staff transferred them to the hospital. The reason for this action was to provide medical supervision to insure their general health and well-being.

On Monday, July 24, Father Berrigan elected to stop the fast and asked to be released from the hospital. Since that time, he has been in regular status. He is now eating, living in regular quarters, and participating in an assigned work program.

Father Berrigan is properly confined at the Lewisburg institution rather than at the minimum security Allenwood Camp for two reasons. Generally, the Allenwood Camp receives prisoners who have sentences of two years or less, or who are within about two years of a firm release date. Father Berrigan has a sentence of six years, and will not be eligible for parole consideration until September, 1971. In addition, Father Berrigan was in fugitive status just prior to his most recent confinement at Lewisburg.

We have discussed Father Berrigan's case with Warden Parker at Lewisburg and are convinced that his treatment is in accordance with our policies. . . .

Judy Poole then telephoned the Federal Bureau of Prisons and inquired about maximum-minimum security regulations, without mentioning Berrigan. Would Carlson's specific interpretation of the Berrigan case match official policy pronouncements? Not exactly. Roger Haney, Assistant Director of Institutional Services of the Federal Bureau of Prisons, said that maximum security is hardly an automatic condition of a more-than-two-year sentence. Age, family ties, and prior criminal record are some of the other factors considered in deciding a prisoner's final status, which ultimately rests on the discretion of the Federal Bureau of Prisons. So Berrigan, as well as Eberhardt and Mische, were being detained in maximum security not because of the rules, but rather according to the will of the Federal Bureau of Prisons. Dan Berrigan's insistence in his "Letter from the Underground" (*New York Review of Books*, August 13, 1970) that Philip was being held in hostage for his own surrender would seem to have corroboration in that admission.

Goodell wrote Carlson again, July 29, referring to Haney's disclosure and suggesting that minimum security would be the more appropriate punishment for Philip Berrigan.

I have received numerous inquiries from individuals who are deeply concerned about the harsh conditions of Reverend Philip Berrigan's confinement.

Your July 27 correspondence stated that Reverend Berrigan is properly confined at the Lewisburg institution first, because he is serving a sentence of greater than two years and second, because he was in fugitive status prior to his most recent confinement. Since receipt of your letter, however, I have been advised that the Bureau of Prisons' regulation regarding minimum security can be superceded at your discretion.

Increased security would seem most appropriate for individuals of a violent nature who might pose a further threat to society. In light of Reverend Berrigan's relentless preaching of nonviolence, his lifelong service to the community, and his announced intention to surrender on the day of his apprehension, Reverend Berrigan's confinement at Lewisburg appears to be a grave injustice.

Due to the above considerations, I strongly request that Reverend Berrigan be placed in minimum security. Your continued interest in this matter is appreciated.

Carlson never wrote back. Events moved too quickly in the next two weeks.

The spiral began when Homer Bigart published a story in *The New York Times* on July 30, headlined "Prison Denies Berrigan Is Mistreated." Since Bigart was not allowed to talk to the prisoners, his report from Lewisburg reflected only Acting Warden Robert L. Hendricks' predictably defensive view of the circumstances surrounding Philip Berrigan's maximum security. Hendricks said extra surveillance was necessary because Berrigan just might try to break out. "Well, hell, he escaped once," he said. Then, contradicting F.B.P. Director Carlson, Hendricks stated that the only reason Berrigan was still in Lewisburg instead of Allenwood Camp—where, Hendricks says, he was scheduled to go in June—was Berrigan's violation of mail regulations. (Berrigan had got a letter past the censors.)

After Bigart filed the story, he called Dr. Gaylin and expressed misgivings concerning the information handed him at Lewisburg. Gaylin had been consulted in the matter of Philip Berrigan several days earlier and was in a position to challenge the witness of Warden Hendricks and the F.B.P. He suggested Bigart talk with Dr. Robert Coles of Harvard for further details. "Dr. Coles? I know Dr. Coles," said Bigart, astonished by the expanding circles of the case. "Is he in this too?" After speaking with Coles, Bigart realized his coverage was grossly misleading. He tried to insert new information into the record but it was too late. *The Times* published the one-dimensional story as he had originally written it.

Coles was furious. "When I saw Bigart's article, I just flipped my lid," Coles said, recalling this frustrating moment in his month-long establishmentarian lobby to remove Berrigan and Eberhardt to safer prison grounds. "Bigart went down to Lewisburg, talked to that warden and wrote a public-relations release. He only had half the story." Coles had the other half—and had come by it most reluctantly.

Robert Coles is a forty-year-old research psychiatrist. After psychiatric training at Harvard, he had worked with Southern blacks who had been improperly imprisoned during the early days of the civil-rights movement, had taught in prisons, and had done medical and psychological examinations of sharecropper families. This research gradually shifted north to Appalachia and then came to rest in Boston where he is now studying white lower-middle-class families.

A group of anxious young Boston doctors had visited him in mid-July to urge him to do something about the situation at Lewisburg. They were disturbed by stories in the press regarding the condition of the two prisoners—Berrigan's harassment and the homosexual threats to Eberhardt. Surely, someone as well respected and well connected as Coles could help. Coles wasn't so certain. "I kept telling them to see psychiatrists more involved in the peace movement because I thought they would be more willing and able to do this. I wasn't sure at that time I could do a damn thing, even if I were willing. But the young doctors wouldn't go away. I told them I was working with lower-middle-class people, conservative Catholics, who were not sympathetic to the Berrigans. What if my name got into the papers on this? This was my particular moral dilemma. I've been on this project for four years. I wasn't pleading a new cause. 'Give me a break,' I said."

The next day Coles was reached by a psychiatrist friend in Philadelphia. "You know, I really think you ought to be ashamed of yourself," said the caller. "They will listen to you." Coles pondered his decision.

"I'm a doctor who has become a kind of social anthropologist," Coles said, confessing the personal anguish brought on by the Berrigan case. "It's hard for me to become identified with an upper-middle-class, university-dominated protest movement. I've been working with middle Americans for four years. If anything, I've been distressed by their problems and their feelings. One just can't leave that and start marching with people who are self-centered, quite arrogant and often interested in problems far away while ignoring their own backyard.

"So before I agreed to go to Lewisburg, I went to see two of the families about Berrigan. Both of the fathers are policemen. They are for the President, intensely angry with the blacks, believe the students are bums. They are still tortured, though. They want out of Asia but with honor. One lost a son in Vietnam and he has to make sense out of that."

The first policeman had no objections. "I don't give a damn what Berrigan is like or what he believes in," he said to Coles. "If he's getting a raw deal in prison, I think that's wrong. But what did he expect? Anyone who goes to jail gets it."

The second policeman was tougher. "You mean Father Berrigan's a Communist." Coles explained some more. "Well, hell," the man said, "he's probably no more Communist than the students at Harvard." Finally the cop gave in by reciting an old but handy Catholic truism, "once a priest, always a priest." He said, "You're a guest of ours, Doctor Coles. Don't worry. Go ahead."

Coles' only acquaintance in the F.B.P. was with retired Director James Bennett. Listening to Coles' polite discourse on Berrigan, Bennett was reminded of the hard times Dave Dellinger gave the F.B.P. in World War II. "Doctor, beware," he said to Coles, "they're going to try to turn this into a political thing." Bennett recommended that Coles take a trip to Lewisburg and examine Berrigan and Eberhardt for himself. Then he would see.

After talking to Bennett, Coles called Dr. Seymour Halleck, a psychiatrist at the University of Wisconsin Medical School, who was well acquainted with the F.B.P. Halleck concurred on the urgency of the case. "Fasting," he said, "can be the beginning of a very serious psychiatric emergency. It escalates. A fast that starts as a protest becomes more than a protest. It becomes a war. The person gets physically sick and mentally broken. It's just a terribly dangerous thing." Halleck told Coles they ought to act on Bennett's suggestion and ask the F.B.P.'s permission to examine Berrigan and Eberhardt.

At this point, Coles consulted Dr. Gaylin. He didn't know Gaylin personally but had reviewed *In the Service of Their Country* for *The New Yorker* and was impressed by Gaylin's views on the penal system. "Three months in maximum security for political prisoners," Gaylin remarked to Coles, "is not only an outrage, but also totally unprecedented." This expert opinion relieved the nagging doubts Coles had retained about his own role in this campaign. "Suddenly, I felt, my God, I'm not walking up some crazy dead-end street. Here was an authority on the subject and he's concerned."

Coles called F.B.P. Director Carlson on July 17 and asked for an appointment with Berrigan and Eberhardt. Carlson was agreeable to a house call at Lewisburg, and the appointment was set for Monday, July 20.

Coles related the story of his experiences on that day.

Gaylin solemnly warned me about Lewisburg but no preparation would have been adequate. It was the most horrible experience. Something Gaylin told me beforehand turned out to be very significant. "Be careful," he said, "that you have spelled out exactly what you're going to do. Because, if you haven't, they'll run circles around you." I asked him what he meant. Carlson already told me everything was arranged. All I had to do was show up there.

"That's not enough," said Gaylin. "You may spend your whole day there without seeing them or seeing them without talking to them under the right circumstances. You're entering Never Never Land at Lewisburg. You've got to watch yourself."

In fact, Coles spent one of the strangest and most unpleasant days of his practice in Lewisburg Federal Penitentiary. Not only was he forbidden to see Berrigan and Eberhardt alone, but in the morning session Associate Warden Hendricks sat in on the interview taking notes. After a half-hour Coles realized the prisoners could not talk freely. Extremely angry, he told Hendricks he was leaving. Hendricks immediately called Warden J.J. Parker, who wanted to talk things over.

The talk, however, became a harangue. Parker screamed at Coles about the troubles he had had with political prisoners. Why do innocent people like him get involved when they don't know what's going on? Didn't he know that the "world is a bad place," that people "must pay for injustice?"

Then he threw a pen at me. He said, "Take this, you'll need it for your notes." I said I had my own pen and put it back on his desk. Then he opened it and showed me a concealed knife.

"You see how dangerous these prisoners are. The man in whose cell we found this pen would appear to you just like Father Berrigan, a nice religious man. This is why we shake down Father Berrigan's cell. This is why we shake down everyone's cell. They are dangerous. They have concealed weapons."

"Are you trying to tell me that Father Berrigan would try to make a knife for himself in this prison and conceal it in a fountain pen?" I said to Parker.

"I'm trying to tell you," he answered, "that I have my problems with security here and I just can't have people like you coming in and out of here talking with these people, feeling sorry for them when we've got some dangerous people here."

"Among whom you count this priest and young poet?"

"Among whom I count everyone that's here."

"Well, I've heard what you have to say and I'm leaving," I said.

"I think you're being very precipitous," the Warden remarked.

"I think I've been too slow protesting," I said. "Furthermore, before I go I want to make my position very clear to the head of the Federal Bureau of Prisons."

Parker called Carlson for me. I told him I found the arrangement at Lewisburg very unsatisfactory.

"I thought we had a very fair arrangement," Carlson said. "I thought it was understood that you were going to talk to the men. I never told you that you were going to talk to them in private."

Eventually a compromise was worked out by telephone between Coles and F.B.P. Director Carlson: the prison doctor would sit in on the interview instead of Warden Hendricks. Thus the morning's aborted interview was resumed for three hours that afternoon.

According to Coles' psychiatric report, both prisoners were in bad shape. For Eberhardt, a continued stay in maximum security meant "the possibility of a severe and seriously impairing, psychotic break." Despite Berrigan's apparent cheerfulness, Coles was alarmed by his confession that "all is not going well." "Men like Father Berrigan," he observed, "do not dramatically collapse, they do indeed gradually lose the kind of well-being, and initiative, and sense of authority about themselves and their values that they have always had. In sum, they lose their dignity."

When the afternoon session was done, Coles visited Parker's office again. There the Warden's macabre harangue began all over again.

I think he was profoundly dumbfounded by my ability to say to him—"Who the hell are you? I can walk out of here today."

He warned me about speeding and said he wouldn't let me go until I accepted a metal serving tray made by the prisoners. I told him I didn't want the tray.

"Sometimes, Doc, the gates don't work around here," he said. You know, macabre.

"I would like nothing better than to spend the night here," I said.

Parker kept at it. So with the serving tray in one hand and my notes in the other, they finally let me out.

I was actually looking out the rear window on the drive back to Philadelphia. After a day there, and Parker's talk about speeding and every other damn thing, I thought, for crying out loud, they'll pick me up. Maybe they want to search me.

You know, you get into a situation like that

—it's Kafka-like—one man standing in the
vestibule, another man taking notes, the warden telling you he may not let you out. You
begin to wonder. . . .

Profoundly disturbed by the gravity of his findings as to the psychological condition of the two
prisoners, Coles spent the rest of that week (July
21–25) trying to enlist the support of doctors and
politicians. Senator Edward Kennedy's administrative assistant, David Burke, was willing to assist but
thought a Republican might be more effective with
the Justice Department these days. (Kennedy did
attempt to intervene with Cardinal Cooke in New
York, a sometime White House Sunday Service
preacher, but the prelate was out of town.) At this
point, Coles linked up with Goodell who, because
he was from Berrigan's home state and an antiwar
Republican, seemed to fit Burke's recommenda-
tion. Coles discovered that Goodell was already
working on the case and would be glad to work in
concert.

Adding to the week's confusion was a most
curious letter Coles received on Wednesday (July
22) from Dr. Norman I. Barr, Chief of Psychiatric
Services at the Federal Bureau of Prisons. Barr's
letter was written the previous Monday, the very
day Coles was at Lewisburg.

Sy Halleck called me this past Friday (July
17) and I'm aware that you are at Lewisburg
Penitentiary today. With such flimsy credentials, I am sending you literature describing
the situation and/or programs during the past
year of nine bureau psychologists, plus a paper
of my own.

My reason for providing you this material
is to provide a perspective which I think you
will be otherwise unaware of. It is easy to crit-

icize government institutions; prisons are the easiest of all. Such criticism often requires little knowledge and no courage, and is destructive in result. But to be constructive requires some degree of both courage and knowledge.

Forgive my pompousness, but I respect your professionalism as exemplified for instance in your paper on Morgantown. It is distressing, however, when people, otherwise knowledgeable, say and write things which are self-righteous, self-aggrandizing, and destructive to their manifest goal.

I trust I have described myself clearly.

Coles called Barr the next day. He did not dwell on the letter, which he considered in bad professional taste, confining conversation instead to Berrigan and Eberhardt, who Barr himself had examined the day before.

"We agreed on the essential psychological facts. Eberhardt was in a state of panic and belonged in minimum security; and he thanked me for using the word 'depression' to describe Berrigan. But then he characterized himself as a bureaucrat, acknowledging that his identification was with the Federal Bureau of Prisons. I think his view was that he was not only concerned with the 'mental health' of these men, but also with keeping up the interests of the bureaucracy."

Despite a rather shocking suggestion by Barr that Berrigan ought to be transferred to another maximum security prison—Atlanta or Leavenworth—in order to contain his "anti-social" and "self-destructive" behavior, Coles was heartened by Barr's essential agreement as to the condition of the two men. "I had the feeling we had won, and so did Gaylin. We thought, okay, they're getting to move those guys to the camp. They know I'm concerned. Barr is worried about Eberhardt in his own way. They had trouble with Phil—where to put him—but we thought it was over. Barr said to call Carlson Monday (July 27) for a decision on the fate of both prisoners."

Coles did call Carlson on Monday the 27th, exactly a week after his trip to Lewisburg. No word yet. Carlson was very cordial and said call back on Wednesday. "I called him on Wednesday and he informed me that they were doing nothing. They had their conference but had nothing to report to me. Suddenly, Carlson was very enigmatic and closed-mouth."

The disappointment with the F.B.P.'s refusal to transfer Berrigan and Eberhardt was followed by gloom when Bigart's story appeared in the *Times* the very next day (July 30). With the bureaucracy and publicity arrayed against them, Coles, who had been holding back so far, was ready and eager to escalate. He leaked some of his findings to *Newsweek* (they appeared August 17). He and Gaylin wrote a joint letter to the *Times* (August 9) which merged Gaylin on the treatment of political prisoners in general and Coles on the specifics at Lewisburg.

Coles then sent copies of his psychiatric reports on Berrigan and Eberhardt to Barr, Carlson, and Attorney General Mitchell. In his accompanying note to Mitchell, he requested an appointment—which was never granted owing to the speedy resolution of the case. But the master stroke in this series of letters was Coles' enclosing his scathing reply to Barr and his letter to Mitchell in the package for Carlson—thus informing the Director of the Federal Bureau of Prisons not only that Coles knew what Barr thought of the two prisoners as a

psychiatrist, but also that the Attorney General
would be apprised of a messy situation in his own
jurisdiction. This became an exquisite squeeze play.

Coles' letter to Barr is not designed to conceal
his rage at a psychiatrist who would minister first
to a bureaucracy and only thereafter to his patients.

> I am replying to your letter of July 20. I
> thought it was a rather unfortunate letter for
> you to send to me. As you yourself indicate, I
> have tried in the past, in many ways, and in
> many articles I have written, to be thoroughly
> fair to the Federal Bureau of Prisons, and in-
> deed have singled out various projects that the
> Bureau of Prisons has undertaken for par-
> ticular praise. I have already spoken to you for
> two hours, from nine thirty to eleven thirty on
> Thursday, July the twenty-third. I hope that as
> a result of our conversation you will not con-
> tinue to think about my visit to Lewisburg in
> the way you seemed tempted to think about it
> in your letter to me. As I explained to you,
> over twenty-five young internists, surgeons, and
> psychiatrists came to see me over a period of
> several days; they all were concerned about
> what was happening to Father Philip Berrigan
> and David Eberhardt, and they asked my help.
> They asked my help because they knew that I
> had been involved in a number of central is-
> sues in this country over the past ten years,
> and to be blunt, they were asking me to do
> this, or perhaps stop writing articles about
> prisons or indeed about many other issues. If
> they are self-righteous, as you are afraid I
> might be, then I can only thank God for that
> kind of self-righteousness; because as you your-
> self acknowledge, there is indeed a need to
> look into some of these difficulties, and in fact
> to be thoroughly critical, in the best sense of
> that word.

With respect to the words "courage" and

"knowledge" that you summoned, I can only say that I have no real interest in calling myself either courageous or knowledgeable—or being called so by you or anyone else. What matters to me in this case, and in many other cases, is whether men are suffering when they should not be suffering, or hurting when they ought not be hurting. The facts are really what we need, and if these facts become bothersome to you, or indeed to me, then perhaps we will look at ourselves as closely and with as much scrutiny as other non-violent dissenters have in the past. I have in mind men like Mahatma Gandhi, Dr. Martin Luther King, and Cesar Chavez. Men like that have also been in prison, and no doubt been both critical, yet full of courage and knowledge.

I don't know whom you have in mind when you talk about "some people, otherwise knowledgeable," who are saying and writing "things which are self-righteous, self-aggrandizing, and destructive to their manifest goal." I wish that you could have been more specific and clear in that particular portion of your letter. Who are those people? How have they been self-righteous? How have they been self-aggrandizing? What destruction have they wrought upon what goals?

I must confess that I am deeply troubled that you should have written the kind of letter you did to me on the very day that I was at Lewisburg, before I had a chance to talk with you, before you had any indication about why I was there or what I might be hoping to accomplish when I arrived there. And since you yourself mention that you had read an article of mine which was thoroughly approving of a major project that the Bureau of Prisons has undertaken in Morgantown, West Virginia, I am even more puzzled by the tone of your letter.

In any event, I am taking the liberty of sending to you two psychiatric reports I have written up; one deals with my impressions about Father Berrigan, the other about David Eberhardt. As you know, we discussed much of this at great length on the telephone. It was my decided impression that essentially we were in agreement; I mean, that you were also concerned about the grave threat to Mr. Eberhardt's psychological condition, and with respect to Father Berrigan, you appreciated the depressive trend in his personality. As I recall, you thanked me for using the word "depression" in evaluating what was happening to Father Berrigan. I also recall that in our conversation you felt that Mr. Eberhardt should be transferred immediately out of Lewisburg Penitentiary, and to either the Allenwood Farm or the Lewisburg Farm. And you agreed with me that a prolonged stay by Father Berrigan in a maximum security prison would be thoroughly detrimental to the man's personality and state of mind.

Now, a week later, the men are still at Lewisburg; and I do wonder what you think physicians like Dr. Willard Gaylin and I ought to do that would be considered by you "constructive."

Next, Coles wanted to have a press conference—the best method, he thought, of smoking out the F.B.P. He told Goodell's assistant, Bob Saks, to inform the Justice Department that he was about to spill the beans at a press conference and had five hundred doctors and ministers ready to march on Washington if Berrigan and Eberhardt were not released from maximum security. Coles would call everything off if the Justice Department came around. Saks did not deliver the message. Instead he called back after talking with Goodell to urge Coles to cool it. Goodell had also written the Attorney General for an appointment with Gaylin and Coles. A press conference or demonstration would destroy any chance of seeing Mitchell and probably make the F.B.P. even more obstinate.

Coles wondered whether he should proceed. He called Ramsey Clark for advice. "Well," Clark said to Coles, "it seems to me you don't want to box them in and they may be getting ready to respond." He offered to call Carlson if Coles thought it might do any good (Coles thought not) and thanked Coles for what he was doing.

The final determination was made late Tuesday afternoon when Saks called back to say that Warden Hendricks had just reported to Goodell's office the decision to transfer Eberhardt to Lewisburg Farm and Mische to Allenwood. Coles cancelled the press conference and waited for the F.B.P.'s next move.

Goodell convinced Coles to hold off a week—until August 12—for an answer from Mitchell on the appointment. If the appointment were denied or if nothing came of it Goodell planned to go to the Senate floor to speak for Philip Berrigan and was counting on the support of Senators Javits, Hatfield, McGovern, and Hughes.

But Daniel Berrigan was caught August 11, on Block Island, twelve miles off Rhode Island's southern coast. That settled the matter immediately (as if the F.B.P. were indeed keeping a bargain with the "hostage"). Assistant F.B.P. Director Haney called Goodell the next day to say that Philip and Daniel Berrigan would be interned in the medium-security Federal Correctional Institution at Danbury, Connecticut, where conditions are not so relaxed as at Allenwood but are a considerable improvement over the maximum security at Lewisburg.

Goodell's low-profile politics and Coles' intelligent improvisations had won. "The real hero in this is Goodell," Coles said, summing things up. "He gave us a day-by-day account of what was going on so that our behavior could be most effective.

"We hear all this nonsense," Coles went on, "about Goodell's part, what he was like before 1968, that he has changed only recently. This attitude is a combination of psychoanalysis and Calvinism. Neither knows what grace means. Each approach traces something back in order to judge the person. Psychoanalysis, for example, always says, But what did you do before? This is why, I think, people can never understand Bobby Kennedy in 1968. They were always trying to judge him by his past. Well, I think the point is to try to get people to change their minds, and if Goodell has changed his mind this way, then, by God, there's hope." Goodell was all this while engaged in his unsuccessful campaign to retain his Senate seat—in which he could not, of course, have been helped by the blessing of the Berrigan brothers.

The Federal Correctional Institution at Danbury is a large rectangular building with an open center court. There are no gun emplacements, no towers, no high walls. Danbury's medium security is afforded rather by an outer ring of administrative offices which wrap around the building. All prisoner activities face the center court. Danbury has a minimum-security reputation, despite its official designation, and a nonviolent population.

While relieved to be out of Lewisburg, Philip Berrigan was not entirely happy with the shift to Danbury. He told Goodell why in a letter dated August 28.

Thank you for your continued, kind efforts. I feel very guilty, in light of the more critical work that you have.

What I'll now mention to you is not an issue—it's merely an attempt at clarification. The Bureau of Prisons neatly dodged issues by this transfer—thereby deflating pressure raised by you and others to have me given normal treatment in minimum security at Allenwood or Lewisburg Farm. They accompanied this by a clever public relations stunt—'we have made exceptions to allow the Berrigans to be imprisoned together.'

Without a doubt, the issue was the possible presence of both of us at Lewisburg Penitentiary, where heat on them could be generated by the question of minimum security, and eventual transfer to Allenwood or Lewisburg Farm, where we might organize other political prisoners. This they could not afford to do.

I am grateful for this move because it gives me the opportunity to see my brother. This fact, however, does not require me to accept the duplicity of the Bureau, and the staff at Lewisburg.

In any case, I intend to play it by ear at Danbury, and see what service I can be to the men here, a high percentage of which are narcotics people. . . .

I realize that portions of this may sound like sour grapes. But both the Bureau and the administration at Lewisburg have repeatedly proven by their actions that they can't endure sustained public scrutiny. Any more than the government can regarding the debacle in Southeast Asia.

Again, many thanks. Dan joins me in best wishes and warmest regards. Peace of Christ!

Francine du Plessix Gray

Phil Berrigan in Hawaii

(Francine du Plessix Gray taped this discussion in Hawaii where she found John and Lucy Witteck and Wayne and Lori Hayashi not yet recovered from the impact of Fr. Berrigan's visit to that island. In the course of this group interview, these two couples disclose their backgrounds and the reasons for their interest in Fr. Berrigan.)

JOHN WITTECK: We're all here to talk about Phil Berrigan, which is hard to do because most of us like to remember him by doing rather than by talking. I met Phil about three years ago in Virginia at a Fellowship of Reconciliation workshop. In those days he was, as always, dynamic, but much more poetic, a much more seemingly gentle nature about him. Those were the days he was working in Baltimore, in a black church with black people. I had been working at State Department and had rather hawkish views, and talking to Phil was the first time that I was really moved by any spokesman on the peace issue. Then last year, in 1969, Phil's book, *Punishment for Peace*, was something we all read in Hawaii, and our friendship with the Catholic theologian, Jim Douglass, who had been teaching at the University of Hawaii, gave us a valuable contact with Phil. So we decided to bring Phil out to Hawaii, and Wayne Hayashi, the most subversive guy in the state, got enough student government monies to bring Phil here. He was the chief agent responsible for that feat.

FRANCINE GRAY: Wayne, can you tell us why you dug Phil's book so?

WAYNE HAYASHI: What impressed me the most about it was his analysis of American society; also his chapter on the color of poverty; his description of Latin America, of how Third World people had been pushed into the margin of humanity; and how we have to see the war in Vietnam from the perspective of the exploited people. The book was really powerful, though some of my friends had difficulty getting through it because it is very heavy reading. It took us quite a while to get Phil to Hawaii because he had to go through the hassle of getting permission to travel from courts and lawyers. And he knew that if he was going to make it, it would be one of his last above-ground speeches, and as it turned out, I think it *was* his last speech above ground . . . after he left us he gave a couple of underground talks before he went to jail.

FRANCINE GRAY: Wayne, let me go back a little bit into your own background. I hear that you're one of the most attacked people on the Japanese language radio stations in Hawaii—you were one of the very first men here who burned his draft card and you were the scandal of the Japanese community. How did you come to have a voice on the student symposium program?

WAYNE HAYASHI: I was in student government at the time. I ran and was elected. I think there's a certain parallel between my decision to stay inside the university structure and the Berrigans' often repeated decision to stay always inside the church, no matter what. I sympathize very much with what Phil and Dan are doing—staying in to awaken the conscience of the Church. I find myself still working with various university programs because the student base is of crucial importance, and what happens on campuses affects the outcome of this world, especially in a state like Hawaii.

FRANCINE GRAY: Three of you—Wayne, Lori Hayashi and Lucy Witteck—are not Catholics. How did you react when you first read about the Catholics leading the far-out fringe of the peace movement? Did you have any particular sympathies for the Catholic Resistance?

LUCY WITTECK: I thought it was strange. When I grew up I always thought Catholics were strange people and I said I would never marry a Catholic. I couldn't see going to Catechism and all this rigid discipline that they're subject to. But when I saw the clippings on Father Dan and Phil and the Catonsville Nine, and we met Jim Forest, I said, "Wow! These guys are really far-out, they're really neat people." And I was impressed and I was very glad, very happy to see that the Catholics were moving. I'd like to see this happen more within the other churches, but John and I have talked about it and we figured that it's because of the discipline of the Catholic Church that the radical element is coming from their group rather than from the Baptists or others.

FRANCINE GRAY: Did you yourself have any religious upbringing?

LUCY WITTECK: I was raised as a Buddhist, but I was baptised in the Southern Baptist Church when I was twelve because my friends were Baptists and it was the closest church to my house. I haven't been there for years and years, and they still send me bulletins, but I was very much on the fringe as far as religion went. I went just because my friends went.

WAYNE HAYASHI: I never really got to know any Catholics growing up in Hilo. The Catholics were the other high school within our district and were archrivals and we hated the Catholics.

FRANCINE GRAY: Did you ever have any gang warfare with them?

WAYNE HAYASHI: There were lots of fights after basketball games and such. I think I visited the Catholic Church once and went to confession with one of my friends, a Chinese boy who was a Catholic, and I thought it was very strange and ornamental. Then in my freshman year at the University of Hawaii I got very interested in existential philosophy and at the same time I began to think about war, poverty, racism. What really turned me on to the Catholic scene was taking a course by Jim Douglass—it was called "Theology of Peace and Revolution." I was very attracted by the man's serious thinking, his commitment to peace, and through him I came to admire people like Fathers Dan and Phil Berrigan, Jim Forest, the Catonsville

Nine. This was in the Spring of 1968—about the same time the Resistance movement grew on our campus. Twelve of us—John Witteck, myself, and ten others—burned our draft cards and Jim Douglass was the guru of the Resistance—also its treasurer!

JOHN WITTECK: He was the first member of the faculty to come to our side.

WAYNE HAYASHI: I started realizing that a lot of the most radical revolutionary people in the movement, nationally and here in Hawaii, were Catholics, came from Catholic backgrounds, and also a lot of them were Southerners like John Witteck, and I was kind of amazed because I thought Catholics were cold people and very sectarian, and not really involved in politics as such. But the Catholic religion has a whole new meaning for me now, and I really respect the Catholics for what they're doing.

FRANCINE GRAY: Did you have any Buddhist training?

WAYNE HAYASHI: Yes, like Lucy, my whole childhood was Buddhist and I went to the Buddhist Church, but I also became a Baptist in junior high school. I went to this revival and got converted for awhile. I'm now an agnostic.

FRANCINE GRAY: Lori, how about you? You probably have a stricter Buddhist training.

LORI HAYASHI: Not really. My parents were never very strict about going to church and teach-

ing me about Buddhism *per se*. But I've been raised
around Buddhism. There are very few theologians,
very few clergymen, who would stand up today; and
to have Catholics in the forefront is just fantastic.
Meeting Phil Berrigan was a great experience. I
really love him, he's just a beautiful person, he's
very warm.

WAYNE HAYASHI: Weren't you afraid of him
also?

LORI HAYASHI: Yes, I was very afraid of him.

WAYNE HAYASHI: Why was that?

LORI HAYASHI: He's such a big man, so tall and
sturdily built. But it's not only his physical aspect,
the way he permeated an aura of strength; it's also
the fact that he seemed to be such a demanding
person, demanding not only of himself but of others,
and that frightened me.

FRANCINE GRAY: What frightened you about it
—the sense that you should be more committed
yourself?

LORI HAYASHI: Right. Because his actions and
those of the Catonsville Nine and other such groups
are so many steps further than anything we'd done.

FRANCINE GRAY: Since some of you have been
brought up in the Buddhist tradition, could you
state what it is in the Buddhist tradition which
would relate to what Phil and Dan Berrigan are
saying?

WAYNE HAYASHI: I think that the Buddhist concept of Karma, of the cause and effect of suffering, is very much related to the message of the Cross as given by Catholics like Jim Douglass, the Berrigan brothers and Jim Forest. Their message to me is what Christianity is all about. The Cross symbolizes suffering. When we see so much human misery throughout the Third World and here in America, we not only have to prevent that suffering, we also have to take that suffering upon ourselves. We have to carry the Cross however heavy it is, and we have to give it some social and political meaning, and this is what the Berrigans have done. I must stress that I too was kind of threatened by the Catonsville action. We had just gotten down to burning our draft cards and taken the first big step and feeling almost self-righteous, you know, this euphoria, and then a month later you pick up the paper and they ripped off a whole draft board, not only their own draft cards, but the whole city's draft board. That was quite a step and we understood it to be the vanguard, pushing on that margin where very few antiwar resisters or pacifists, very few men or women, dare tread on . . . the unknown, and they took that step and many followed in their path and were really admired. And yet at the same time we were threatened by this kind of action because it raised the ante, raised the stakes. Meeting Phil was not like meeting a priest, but like meeting a military man, a general or a guerilla leader. And what more can I say except his life is his message, and you feel very small when you're with him. Wow, you feel like you have to do more.

FRANCINE GRAY: Do you think that people like Phil and Dan make up in a certain kind of psychological violence what they lack in physical violence, that this way they have of making you feel insufficient and guilty is a form of psychological violence? Let's discuss that a bit: the violence of martyrs.

JOHN WITTECK: Yes, I think that's true. Phil especially comes through like that, like an avenging angel, which is great. In my process of development certain people have represented certain things to me: Kennedy, youthful vigor and idealism in a secular way; Pope John, age-old compassion and the insights of the old, which is so close to that useful vigor of the young. They both died within a few months of each other, left us without anybody. And Martin Luther King woke me up to what Christianity meant . . . loving your enemy. He was killed. And then I guess it was the Berrigans who awoke me to Christian justice and for once I felt proud of the Church too. For the first time the Offertory had some meaning, when the blood was poured on the draft files. Somebody was really offering his life for other men and the whole Mass became significant, the whole idea of community became very significant again. It wasn't just that once-a-week-on-Sunday social gathering in which everybody watched how other people dressed or behaved. Berrigan brought back the sense of justice, which is a merciless kind of thing, a violent kind of thing. But he offered us for the first time, after Pope John, Kennedy and King, some kind of clue as to how to put this into action; and I think Berrigan's book, *Punishment for Peace*, was the first one really to relate poverty and racism to the whole international spectrum. I think the great hope for all of us is if all the avenging angels can get together: the Panthers and the Catholic Resistance and the Third World struggle groups. I think we know the problems now. We have some clues to forming communities of action, and a person like Phil shames us into doing because we all know what has to be done. And that does do violence because what he's calling you to do is going to cause a hell of a lot of suffering. It's going to cause you separation from the people you love, it might even cause you death. But when you hear somebody like Phil or Dan just lay out the picture, then its alternatives are much better than the alternatives of inaction, and you don't really have a choice.

FRANCINE GRAY: What they do is kind of create a new center of gravity for us.

JOHN WITTECK: Right.

FRANCINE GRAY: And that's very disturbing because we're thrown off balance. Could you describe how the peace community in Hawaii reacted to Phil? How many people did you get to meet with him and hear him, what were the different levels of reaction?

JOHN WITTECK: There were probably 200 people at the Church of the Crossroads in Honolulu, which had been the scene the previous summer of the largest sanctuary in the country—37 A.W.O.L. G.I.'s got sanctuary in that Church. And Phil also talked to a class of 200 students at the University of Hawaii, and he talked later that afternoon to 400–500 people, and I think they were all disturbed because he didn't come and give us answers. He usually spoke from a prepared text and he just told us what we knew. It's what he didn't say that really bothered us. "What do we do, Phil?" "Give us the word." "We'll follow you." "Don't go to jail." "Don't leave us in Hawaii." That's what we all were trying to say to him. And I think we put some doubts in his head about going to jail, but unfortunately the airline strike didn't come off and he got away from us.

FRANCINE GRAY: You mean you were actually trying to get him to go underground in Hawaii?

JOHN WITTECK: Yes. We need that nonviolent guerilla that people can have almost absolute faith in.

FRANCINE GRAY: Did he give a different talk to each of the groups or was it more or less the same?

WAYNE HAYASHI: Different. And the thing that disturbed a lot of people was that Phil was so straightforward. Earlier that Spring Dick Gregory had come, a lot of jokes, wet, wry humor, and Dave Dellinger and Jerry Rubin had followed a month later. All hard-hitting speakers, but Phil— his message was that he had done what he had done and he was probably headed for a long jail sentence. It was a torture to sit there listening to this beautiful man who was headed for prison. Here we were free, and at this time in America I don't think we can afford to enjoy that kind of anarchistic freedom. Phil gave us the sense that whenever we're not in trouble facing courts, facing jail, that means we're not being effective. That's what disturbed a lot of people—the sense that we all had to do so much more.

FRANCINE GRAY: Can you describe how Phil affected different people in the Catholic community in Honolulu?

JOHN WITTECK: We had a very late night meeting with several Catholics at our house. What happened mainly is that Phil listened to everyone apologizing for not doing enough. It must have been very frustrating for Phil.

WAYNE HAYASHI: Must have sounded like Confession.

JOHN WITTECK: Yes, for once the Sacrament of Penance had some real meaning. Monsignor Daniel Dever—he's the Superintendent of Catholic schools here—explained what he's trying to do within the system to effect changes and hold off the repression, and Phil just kept nodding his head. Another member of the group, a doctor, explained that with families, several kids, commitments, insurance, how can you take that kind of risk? I remember myself trying to explain what I was doing, which was trying to get people ready for what Phil had done. It *was* like a Confessional. Phil coming here, I think, wrecked the movement and made us very dissatisfied with what we were doing, with leaflets and all that. The Resistance underwent a kind of slow death after that. We weren't doing what we knew we had to do. Almost all the other liberal peace groups folded. Until the Cambodian invasion we weren't resuscitated. And that was quite a different thing than the Berrigan thing. It was like going back before Berrigan. So there is a tendency in Hawaii to say, "Well, something's passé on the mainland"—those kinds of draftboard actions, in which property is destroyed. But I think this is our cop-out. I think the effect of people like the Berrigans, Jim Douglass and Jim Forest had taken root in people and it's going to come out, in a delayed reaction.

FRANCINE GRAY: I feel that we're very devoid of leadership now that the Berrigans are in jail.

JOHN WITTECK: They were one of the new national voices that almost all the kids listened to: The SDS kids, the Resistance, the Third World groups. They seemed to be respected by almost all factions, and now their voices are quieted.

WAYNE HAYASHI: One of Phil's biggest impacts on my politics was his emphasis on small communities of action . . . he talked of sometimes driving five hundred miles in one night to see just "one real person," as he put it. This had a tremendous impact on us all, the idea of building little communities of action, collectives. And Phil talked about developing a kind of collective relationship in which you not only agree with each other's politics and ideology, you also trust and love each other, so that when the action becomes heavy, when the risks are escalated, you can still work together to survive. Because when the ship gets heavy, it's important that you can trust each other to the point that you know each other's limitations, weaknesses and strengths. This is one of the key points we learned from his short visit here and it made a big impression on us.

FRANCINE GRAY: John, you were praising the jail-going experience of the Berrigans, but I have also heard you praise Dan Berrigan's underground experience. Don't you think some of us are rather torn about that?

JOHN WITTECK: I don't think you can be absolute. Some people have to prove the seriousness of their action by going to jail, others have to prove it by refusing to submit to authorities. I think that Phil talks to a different group of people than Dan did. You have to reach people in different ways. Right now one of the ways we're trying to reach people in Hawaii is through the Catholic Church, which is the biggest single organized religion in the state. Over 30 percent of the islanders are Catholic. We want to talk about land issues, housing, rents, the military, Rest and Recreation, education —all these issues—through a Catholic perspective. People have been questioning the Resistance here in the past months . . . what are you doing, they ask, how come there's no peace march this year so we can do our token thing, how come there's no letters to the editor drive, no Resistance fund raising, how come none of your people are going to jail, what are you doing for peace? But we don't feel that's where the action is anymore.

FRANCINE GRAY: Where do you feel it's at?

JOHN WITTECK: Well, here in Hawaii—and we talked to Phil a lot about this—we feel that most people can't be reached on the war issue alone anymore. We have to bring the war home in terms of issues they can relate to. Land, for instance. The same people who own most of the land in Hawaii are some of the biggest war contractors on the islands—American Factors, Castle and Cooke, Dillingham. And the military owns or controls 56 percent of the land on this island. These firms and the military are making it miserable for every-body—for Hawaiians, Filipinos, students. If the Hawaiians see that it's the poor people and the nonwhites who are getting messed up by these holders of power and wealth, then they can protest a war which drafts their sons to fight other non-white people for more profits. I think Phil had some questions about this approach because of the immediacy of the war issue. We still do peace or-ganizing, draft resistance work, etc., but not solely and exclusively. It has to be in the broader con-text of what Hawaii is.

FRANCINE GRAY: Did Phil relate the movement in Hawaii to the movement at large, did he specify the kind of work that he thought had to be done here?

JOHN WITTECK: Not that much. A lot of people who come from the mainland try immediately to relate to Hawaii and tie its problems in. But Phil was here more to learn, so we tried to fill him in. Anybody who comes here is right away struck by both the beauty and the prostitution of the place and the heavy emphasis on the military. Phil might have mentioned that, but his main point was that community is possible anywhere among people of good will and Hawaii is no different than Baltimore.

FRANCINE GRAY: The four of you, the Hayashis and the Wittecks, have been living together for some months or a year?

WAYNE HAYASHI: Two years.

FRANCINE GRAY: Was there any conscious idea on your part that this kind of community life would make it easier on the women if one of you had to go to jail?

LORI HAYASHI: It's funny. Right after Jim Forest was here, there was this feeling that the guys would go down to the draft board the next day and burn draft cards. We were really thinking that. And Lucy and I had been talking about how nice it would be if we had each other.

JOHN WITTECK: You were ready to write us off.

LORI HAYASHI: Right. I think it would be a lot easier, having somebody to relate to who's experiencing something very similar to what you are. You could understand and sympathize.

JOHN WITTECK: Phil had little faith that married men could undertake his kind of commitment, action, and I think we're still out to prove him wrong and will. He was critical that, for instance, in the D.C. Nine some relationships were formed that may have hurt the discipline of the group. That's one good argument for celibacy in the Catholic priesthood. And maybe that's what the Catholic Church can do for the movement. We have the tradition of fasting and celibacy, we have the disciplines that used to seem very silly to me as a young Catholic, but they're taking on some new meaning.

FRANCINE GRAY: It will help keep the population down, too.

WAYNE HAYASHI: Lori and I had our first baby, a girl, just two weeks ago. We believe in building the movement not only through organizing, but also through babies.

JOHN WITTECK: Lucy and I named our baby after Phil, hoping that he will grow up like his namesake.

FRANCINE GRAY: What is his full name?

JOHN WITTECK: Matthew Iwizaku Berrigan Witteck. Iwizaku means "Rock of Peace." So Phil did leave a baby behind even though he's celibate.

WAYNE HAYASHI: There's one last thing I'd like to mention about Phil which impressed me so— this man seems absolutely incapable of fear.

JOHN WITTECK: Absolutely incapable of any fear except the fear of the Lord.

FRANCINE GRAY: Same with Dan Berrigan. We must always remain aware of that moment in Dan's testimony at the trial of the Catonsville Nine when he was talking about a trip he'd made to South Africa, and he was meeting with a group of citizens who were protesting *apartheid*, and one of them asked him, "Father, what happens to our children if we go to jail?" Dan turned to this person and answered: "What happens to your children if you *don't* go to jail?"

JOHN WITTECK: Right on, Dan!

WAYNE HAYASHI: AKAMAI, Phil! That's Hawaiian for "right on."

Jim Forest

Philip
Berrigan:
Disturber
of Sleep

I have the impression that I first met Phil Berrigan on the back of a Wheaties box when I was twelve—a human antelope gliding over mountainous linebackers like a paper airplane in an updraft. Later encounters took place on television: he was town marshal in Dodge City; he was the tough, secretly pious coach at Notre Dame; he was (precursor of Snoopy) a downed American R.A.F. volunteer working with the French resistance. . . .

My more factual memories of Phil begin in late November, 1961, when a fat envelope from New Orleans arrived at St. Joseph's, a house of hospitality on the New York Bowery which serves as well as the editorial office for the penny-a-copy monthly, *The Catholic Worker*. I was assigned to prepare for Christmas publication the packet's contents—a long essay on Christianity and racism from Father Philip Berrigan, S.S.J. (The initials, I immediately learned from another editor, stood for the Society of St. Joseph, an American order founded after the Civil War to serve blacks.) At the time, Phil was teaching at a totally black New Orleans Catholic high school.

Already he was known as a disturber of the sleep.

Witness an incident described in that *Catholic Worker* essay. Though described as if it involved another priest, I learned several years later that the experience was Phil's own:

> Recently . . . a young priest was sent to a "White" parish to offer two Masses on a Sunday . . . In the Gospel, Our Lord was tested by a Doctor of the Law, and from the encounter came the two great Commandments of Love. The priest came armed to preach on this text with an application to the injustice of segregation. He quoted his text and the words of Christ saying that on these two commandments depend the whole Law and the Prophets, and he was getting nicely launched into his sermon, when there came an abrupt disturbance from the congregation. A man was on his feet in the middle of the church, waving his arms excitedly and shouting toward the pulpit, "Hey! I didn't come here to listen to this junk. I came to hear Mass."

The man, with others, finally walked out, shouting back, "If I miss Mass today you're responsible!"

At length Phil concluded his reflection,

> . . . we show no reluctance in noising about the claims of the Church, we suffer no arbitration of her deposit of truth, we glibly repeat the lofty message of Our Lord, but in the desperately important encounter with those who need us, in the hard and hot work of the vineyard where hope is extended, truth exchanged, solidarity and brotherhood won—it is here that we fall, or fail to be present . . . If the

challenges of our age seem too much for us, if we insist on reliving the 19th Century, then we ought to question our religion, we ought to renounce our Western culture and the democracy that is so much a part of it, we ought to maintain that God has no part in this world of His, because we have refused Him entrance. And I know that we will refuse to do this.

It was several years before I began to measure, in the experience of friendship, the extraordinary seriousness with which the author had long been speaking. By then *Pacem in Terris* and the life of Pope John were upon us, and Dan and Phil were among the cornerstones of the emerging Catholic Peace Fellowship. Facts about Phil were beginning to accumulate.

Irish father, German mother; born in 1923 in the pioneer country of the Minnesota Iron Range; the youngest of Thomas and Frieda's six sons; father Thomas, railroad engineer, fired (family witnesses disagree) either for his union activism and socialist convictions, or for reading poetry on the job; early memories of bitter winters and of hospitality extended to the human ruins of the Depression years; the buying of a farm and the move to Syracuse, New York; devout family, authoritarian nuns; a star athlete in high school; a summer of scouring steam engines in a Syracuse round house in order to go to St. Michael's College, Toronto, in the fall of 1942.

Then the draft, with training in the South that brought with it experiences of racism and poverty —a meal of buzzard stew; and then the war in Europe, the seeing of gutted cities, the experience of death and of death-making; a battlefield commission in the artillery.

After forty months in the war, Phil became a student again, this time at the Jesuits' College of the Holy Cross. In 1950 he entered the Josephite Seminary, the third Berrigan brother to seek out ordination. ("To my brother, Father Dan, S.J., without whom neither my priesthood nor this book would be possible," reads the dedication of Phil's first book, *No More Strangers*.) By 1960, with an M.A. from Xavier University in New Orleans, he was well into the business, with words at least, of disturbing the sleep.

By 1963, the words were beginning a pilgrimage toward more bodily expression: Phil arrived in Jackson, Mississippi, to join a sit-in protesting bus segregation. Paged at the airport, he found the local bishop on the phone: either Phil left immediately, or Josephites working in that diocese would be ordered out. Phil was checked, but the event was front-page news the following day; once again the religious dimensions of a secular crisis were being unfolded. While some were grumpy with the alarm clock that was waking them to such dimensionality, it would be a long time before sleep could again be so anesthetized and dreams so barren.

In 1964, Dan, Jim Douglass, and I had gone on from meetings with priest-workers and others in Paris, to Rome, Zurich, and finally Prague where a world conference of peace-concerned Christians, not many of them Catholic, was gathering. In the course of the weeks together, a resolve was born to form a new vehicle for Catholic peace education, conscientious objector support—even the development of nonviolence in spirit and action; out of it the Catholic Peace Fellowship began, and

with that Phil became one of the most immediate
figures in my life.

Though Phil had been absent on our European
journey, his dual commitment to Catholicism and
life-affirming social change disposed us to agree
he would be the ideal one to chair the Catholic
Peace Fellowship. I wrote Phil, as did Dan, with
the proposal. The response was strong and positive, but a major modification was insisted upon:
"It would be good to have a layman in charge—
it may be something of an education to clerics in
general." (We ended up with a co-chairmanship
that included Phil, Marty Corbin of the Catholic
Worker, Tom Cornell, and myself; Dan was put
on the sponsors list, not because he was less active
in the leadership than Phil, but because it seemed
peculiar to have two Berrigans—neither of them
widely known—jostling each other at the top of
the letterhead.)

Finally, that year, we met. Phil was spending
the summer at a Josephite residence in the Bronx,
a high-ceilinged, immaculate rectory with enormous portraits of Roman pontiffs on the parlor
walls, a vast, beer-and-steak-laden-kitchen—and a
warrior of a cook who presided, so it seemed, over
a great deal more than food.

I had no preparation for Phil's appearance. I
generally expected a certain softness in priests,
even those of prophetic tonality. But here was
Phil: tall, striding, blue-eyed, with a powerful,
calm handshake, a Gary Cooper grin and—sur-
prisingly for the junior among the Berrigan brothers—thoroughly gray hair. There certainly were
no broader shoulders on General Patton or at
Notre Dame. And though we had never met, the

style was family reunion, as at a St. Patrick's Day home feast.

His room, in sharp contrast to a dustless order elsewhere in the house, was cluttered and rumpled. Most astonishing were the mountain ranges of books, newspapers and magazines—stacks of I. F. Stone *Weeklies, The New Republic, The Nation, Commonweal,* ripped-up issues of *The New York Times, The Wall Street Journal, The Washington Post,* and so on. Exclamation marks were noticeable in margins; whole paragraphs were underlined. It was my first—certainly not the last—glimpse of Phil's hunger for data and analysis. Tom Cornell, who had come with me, commented on leaving, "Now *there* is someone who does his homework!"

We were struck as much by the dissimilarity between the two brothers—not merely a physical discrepancy, but a difference invading every zone of their lives other than their shared recognition of religious and historical priorities. Dan's quarters (then in a Jesuit town house that had once been Emily Post's) was a carefully assembled collage of signs, artwork, posters, books and furnishings that made the room kaleidoscopic—a visual poem. It was the difference between dame and *dame,* or Gallo and Chateauneuf du Pape. Dan was stamped, inside and out, with France; and Phil with the driving style of American football and board chairmen. It was an unprecedented, impossible partnership.

In the fall came a tougher experience of Phil as coach. He and Dan had been among several pressing me to give up my livelihood, journalism, in order to turn the C.P.F. into a full-time, staffed organization; for my part, I was quite willing to

stop newspapering, but for different purposes: a
recurrent bout with fears of future economic in-
security had convinced me that it was necessary
to get a degree—certification authorizing survival,
it seemed. In fact, I had studied and taken the
college boards, and a quite good small college had
offered full tuition and a living allowance in response to my letter and the test results; my days
as a high school dropout seemed finally numbered.
Phil promptly heard of this and, not enthused at
all, set a date—we would meet in Manhattan the following afternoon. We walked for a bit, settled in
at an Irish bar, ordered some rye, and began to
argue. Formal education, he declared with no uncertainty, was an unfortunate necessity for many,
but a better education was available, for those
willing to do their homework, in the movement;
indeed, only in the fray could there be a meaningful linking up of the data and speculation of
study with the overwhelming fact of needless human suffering and waste; and only in such a
context could hope have any substance. "You've
got more education already than you'll ever get
in school, and you're getting more daily. Those
certifications aren't worth the paper they're
printed on. Get in the movement, stay in the movement, stick with it."

His message was largely in harmony with Bob
Dylan's, "The only difference between schools and
old-age homes is that more people die in schools."
I was by no means without replies, and deeply
felt they were, as at the time I could see little
but poetry in Jesus' suggestion that I consider the
lilies of the field and think not on the morrow.
But Phil was not only determined but persuasive;
my final consent to give the C.P.F. a trial run

of six months full-time work resulted in considerable Berrigan joy, signaled by a solid whack on his leg, an exclamation of, "That's the spirit, man!" and several additional rounds of rye.

Phil is a disarming man. While his convictions are achieved by a patient route and are solidly clung to once established, the style of personal expression is less chancery-dogmatic than akin to Spencer Tracy's portrayal of Father Flanagan of Boys' Town. "Love ya, man," was a phrase that often preceded the closing in his constant letters; the closing itself invariably made reference to the focal point of Phil's commitment—"The Lord's Peace," "In Christ," "In Xto," "Fraternally in Him," "The Savior's Inspiration and strength. . . ." As we became closer, he more frequently dropped the *Fr.* from his signature, but the S.S.J. never was pruned away.

Phil has areas of considerable shyness and silence. He is most noticeably mute regarding his involvement in World War II—I have never once heard him make reference to that experience; it is like a crypt within a pyramid. My first awareness of his commissioned veteran status came from the dust jacket of *No More Strangers*. But if there is, as it seems, a special, silencing pain about that zone of his life, it is but the most extreme example of a general reticence about utilizing his own biography in articulating his convictions. Hence his casting the sermon described in *The Catholic Worker* as if it were the experience of another.

Phil is wonderfully conservative in many respects. Chesterton's reverent definition of orthodoxy could be Phil's: "Tradition is democracy extended through time. It is *the* universal suffrage:

it is giving the vote to one's ancestors." In matters
liturgical, few priests were more disinterested in
change; Phil had been interested in the 1950's,
to the point of publication in *Worship* magazine
of an essay relating liturgy and the needs of the
black community. But in the 1960's Dan's gift
and passion in liturgical innovation begins to
stand in nearly total contrast. I have the recollection that it was Phil who first mentioned to me,
with no small disgust, that the Church in Germany
prided itself on its liturgical and theological re-
newal during the years of human-fed ovens.

Phil is often angry with high churchmen. When
Bishop (now Cardinal) Wright politely backed
off making a statement on the virtue of resistance
to the Vietnam war (though Wright had made
public his strong dissent against the war), Phil's
comment was, "He hasn't been out in the rain
alone since he was four." Yet his angers and disappointments with hierarchial spokesmen have
never reduced his conviction that there were
grounds for especially high expectations from the
Church—"that is, you and me," as he adds. For
him, "the Church" meant Catholic, in which regard Phil made no bones about being Roman, but
his definition was encompassing. He quotes Bishop Gerard Huyghe of Arras:

> That man is Catholic (Christian) who opens
> himself to all and allows the universal love
> of the Lord to resound in his heart. He is a
> Catholic who, when he remembers the mercy
> of Christ toward him, becomes merciful—
> that is to say, overwhelmed with distress,
> whatever form that distress may take. He is a
> Catholic who instinctively rejects everything
> that is a source of division, who cannot meet
> anyone without tirelessly seeking out an area

of agreement. He is a Catholic who sees in each man not the social category to which he belongs, not the label which is applied to him, of unbeliever or Protestant or Jew or Communist, but the brother for whom Christ died and who has been placed in his path in order to receive his love. He is a Catholic who through humility, has made himself poor in spirit and is always ready to welcome those who are deprived, whether it be of material goods or the light of faith.

Few so well synthesize, in the context of faith, the seeming antitheses of action and contemplation. There is no forgetting Phil's stillness during several days at the Abbey of Gethsemani in Kentucky in the summer of 1965. We—Dan, Phil, A. J. Muste, W. H. Ferry, John Howard Yoder, Tom Cornell, Bob Cunnane and several others— were there at Thomas Merton's invitation to explore together the "spiritual roots of protest." Merton saw our gathering as occurring "in the face of the injustice and disorder of a world in which total war at times seems inevitable, in which few seek any but violent solutions." I recall Phil sitting in Merton's cinder-block hermitage, absolutely calm and intent, in T-shirt and black trousers, a Quakerly silence about him. My only clear memories of Phil breaking his meditative quiet during those three days were first when I sought him out one night, for confession, and later, with the group, when he looked for parallels to our own situation in the Hitler years. In the first, the overwhelming impression surviving now is of Phil's surprising gentleness and his stress on the relationship between penitance and hope. When he spoke with the group, it was finally of Franz Jägerstätter, the Austrian peasant-farmer and de-

vout Catholic (one-time motorcyclist) who, against
all advice from churchmen and friends, had resisted Hitler's wars to the point of his own be-
heading. Merton's own appreciation of the fusion
of reflection and resistance within Phil is suggested by his dedication to Phil of *Faith and Violence*, the last book by Merton published before
his death.

The going with Phil was not always easy. While
no one did more to keep the Catholic Peace Fellowship financially afloat, nor cared more personally for the well-being of his friends, there were
times of considerable discord.

The most severe strain came after the blood-
pouring action in Baltimore in November, 1967.
A long chain of events had led up to that experiment—years punctuated with speeches all over
the country, countless meetings with senators, administration officials, generals and bishops, peaceful invasions of military installations, vigils in
front of the homes of members of the Joint Chiefs
of Staff, intense efforts to prod Congress to hold
hearings on the illegality and immorality of the
Vietnam war. The results convinced Phil that
petitionary nonviolence had been proved, after the
most sincere and concerted efforts, to be futile;
the time had come for militant, nonviolent resistance—and the blood pouring was the first
event that concretely declared that realization. But
having made that anguished crossing, along with
Tom Lewis and several others, some of us who
had been on pilgrimage with him year upon year
suddenly seemed in the B.C. division of his new
commitment. He wrote December 2,

[My criticism is] slowly and reluctantly spoken,
mainly because I abhor hurting friends, some-

times to the point of cowardice. But . . . I had better say . . . what I think.

My impression has been, for well over a year, that the Fellowship of Reconciliation [a large, religiously oriented pacifist group not drawn toward acts of civil disobedience, with which the Catholic Peace Fellowship was closely affiliated] has moved steadily to the margin of the war-peace issue. Frankly, I no longer take it seriously; and I take the CPF seriously only because I love and respect my friends who are in it. Not because it is realistically facing Vietnam and/or the Cold War.

Now it may be, and I'm ready to admit this, that people in both organizations are doing their utmost, and doing it conscientiously. That's their affair. But in face of what this war has become, with its contribution to probable nuclear war—they are out of it. Tom [Cornell] says that the movement must be orchestrated. Perhaps. But the term reminds me of white liberal jargon—jargon used by people who still will be building their broad base [of support in society] as the Bombs come in. I will refuse to indict anyone's conscience, but I don't have to cheer their work, which seems to me safe, unimaginative, staffish and devoid of risk or suffering.

. . . [Dan and I] have been led to different roads, ones which seem to us more at grips with this awful war and the insanity of our country. To stop this war, I would give my life tomorrow, and I can't be blamed if I have little time for those who want to run ads in the New York Times . . . Both Dan and I are seriously dealing with clergymen and laymen, professionals and family people, who have come to the point of civil disobedience and the prospect of jail, and are even foundering with convictions beyond that point. As Johnson continues to have his war, and that means the probability of invading North Vietnam, we will either witness from jail, or we will go ahead with social disruption, including non-violent attacks against the machinery of this war . . .

In a word, I believe in revolution, and I hope to continue a nonviolent contribution to it. In my view, we are not going to save this country and mankind without it. And I am centrally concerned with the Gospel view that the massive suffering of this war and American imperialism around the world will only be confronted by people who are willing to go with suffering as the first move to justice.

. . . I hope this clears up more than it obscures. Whatever the case, you will continue to mean much to me as a friend and teacher. Christ's love and peace.

The letter occasioned pain and anger. Failing to catch its real tonality, it seemed instead self-righteous and arrogant. Today what is most striking is its gentleness and love, persistent despite my own fear and the superficiality of my own response to the Land of Burning Children, as Dan was to rename Vietnam at Catonsville.

So at last, I too was the one in the church, angry with the preacher for his incursions upon my frightened, strait-jacketed conscience. My response was not qualitatively dissimilar to the parishioner shouting as he left, "If I miss Mass today, it'll be your fault!"

Now Phil is in prison and I, draft-record burner, have recently attained the status of ex-convict. On the East Harlem streets outside Emmaus House there is just now a furious honking, ironic counter-point to prison, of a trapped car's attempt to escape a captivity established by another's double-parking. Through adjacent doors there is a muted urgency in women's voices as they explore, as they do each week here, the meaning of their experience as women. Later tonight there will be a public reading here of Dan's poem-rendering of the Catonsville trial transcript. Tomorrow there will be preparatory work on classes—one dealing with urban problems and another on the lessons to be drawn from earlier nonviolent revolutionary struggles. There will be as well the purchasing of some tolerable wine and bread, some reading from Robin Hood and C.S. Lewis' children's tales, renewed Lenten wrestling with the balky beast of self . . . .

And again there will remain the urgency and the questioning of Phil Berrigan's life. And it will be all the stronger for a discovery borne of these recent days of remembering and writing and re-reading (as if for the first time) some of what has ended up in these paragraphs. The discovery: that even someone like myself, officially of the resistance, a certified felon of the divine disobedience tradition, can continue to disguise fear as insight, and practice a defensive arithmetic of the sort that carefully and infallibly demonstrates that bumblebees are incapable of flight. And that sleepers, especially this one, can't awake. That we're better asleep. That it is a virtuous sleep. That it is a helpful sleep, a Christian sleep. That it is a wakeful sleep.

But the alarm clock of a Wheaties-box priest insists on ringing, annoyingly keeps ringing, persists and persists in its insistence of the time.

Paul Cowan

Father Dan
Berrigan:
Fugitive
from Injustice

Father Daniel Berrigan has been part of the authentic American underground for more than a
month now—ever since he refused to submit to a
legal system that sentenced him to three and one-
half years in jail for napalming some draft files in
Catonsville, Maryland. Since then, he has been
"reading, writing, and studying," and traveling
from city to city "paying quick visits on old
friends." His most dramatic appearance and get-
away was at a freedom seder at Cornell, but he
must have had a hundred more intimate rendezvous. For he believes that an underground movement must have links with a legitimate political
movement: "We have to take our chances with
those within the law. Many liberals are frustrated
and want to help."

Recently he was in New York, and a mutual
acquaintance suggested that I talk to him for *The
Voice.** We spent two hours together: it's been
years since I met anyone whose example forced
me to think so seriously about the way I live my
own life.

The Village Voice (a New York weekly).

We met in the sort of modest, neat New York walk-up apartment that thousands of *Voice* readers must live in. Some day very soon, if America continues in the direction it seemed headed last week, your apartment, too, might be part of an underground network. From what I could gather, Berrigan would meet a few people there, a few people elsewhere, then leave the city.

Berrigan's brother Philip had been arrested in Manhattan several days before we met, and he was clearly preoccupied with that event. For example, shortly after we met I asked him whether the act of going underground had allowed him to find a sort of peace within himself. Of course, the question reflected the torment that so many of my friends and I feel as we continue to lead relatively normal lives inside a country that is destroying so much of the world. But it failed totally to comprehend his hunted reality.

"I could be certain of how much peace I feel if I were more practiced at this life. But my peace could be ripped apart by two F.B.I. agents at any moment. So I must be modest when I talk about myself. I must be sure that I'll be equally at peace in the West Side Jail. Still I want to take every precaution to keep this thing going."

But if his mood was watchful, his manner was calm. My twenty-month-old daughter Lisa was with me when I went to his apartment, fussy with midday fatigue. I was afraid her crying would jar his nerves, but instead he began to help me soothe her immediately and then to calm a jumpy cat which threatened to shatter her nap. I felt like a proud, slightly incompetent father who'd decided to spend a sweet Saturday showing his child off to a cherished older friend—for a moment it was impossible for me to accept the fact that the gentle man in the room with me was a fugitive from American justice.

He did not seem so much like an American, frantic and full of grand plans, as he did like the North Vietnamese whom travelers who have come to love that country often describe. "I found so much over there to help me," he says of his own trip to Hanoi during which he helped bring about the release of three captured American pilots. During much of our interview he sat in a lotus position, answering each of my questions slowly and searchingly. Though his eyes frequently teared with fatigue (he is forty-eight, and following a schedule that would exhaust a twenty-year-old), he remained sensitive to every nuance of mood and discussion.

At one point he interrupted the interview to get each of us a glass of water—it was almost a ceremony—and then, with genuine concern about his capacity to explain himself to *Voice* readers, asked: "How am I doing?" The question made me review the entire process of interviewing, which always makes me uncomfortable, and I suggested that he talk to readers in his own voice by writing his own article for the paper. "I can't. I might have to leave town very hastily," he said. "Go ahead. You're doing fine."

He is a tall, slender man with warm eyes and a voice that retains the gentle lilt of his youth in rural Minnesota: it is easy to imagine the same frame housing a successful farmer or a beloved country judge. This decade, and Berrigan's response to its horrors, has turned him into one of the wisest, most patient Americans I've ever met.

Talking with him now, one tends to imagine that

his risky, principled decisions come easily, instinctively—blacks have natural religion, Jesuits are naturally ascetic and moral. But the fact is that Father Berrigan has had to rely on the nerve ends of his will to make his life consistent with his beliefs: he has re-created himself to suit the times.

In 1962, after a meeting at the Fellowship of Reconciliation, Dorothy Day of the *Catholic Worker* said of him, "Wasn't that Berrigan just like a priest. Talk, talk, talk, and doesn't give anyone else a chance to open their mouth." (The remark is quoted in Francine du Plessix Gray's excellent profile of the Berrigan brothers in *The New Yorker*, March 14, 1970.)

A year in France changed him some—friends from that period usually recall that he looked like a French worker priest, and often describe him with a sack of wine flung jauntily over his shoulders. He and Philip began their sharp battles with the church shortly after he returned, and at one point Daniel's superiors tried to exile him to South America because he insisted on speaking out against the war. But pressure from younger Jesuits forced them to bring him back to the United States.

At Cornell, though, he was relatively cautious for several years: he frequently urged students to risk jail by resisting the draft while he retained a secure berth as a member of the University's faculty. Like so many literary radicals in New York, he was gaining prominence as a spokesman for a movement that was sustained by other people's risks. (His poetry from that time, which he includes in "Real Men, False Gods," seems a little precious and removed, reflecting his role.) That contradiction must have tormented him, but he did

not participate in Philip's first draft board action,
where four men poured blood over some files.
(Instead, he chose to go to jail during the Pentagon demonstration—that is the plane of courage
and cowardice he forces one to write on.)

At first he was reluctant to get involved in the
Catonsville raid, which Philip also helped inspire.
Then, according to Francine Gray's article, the two
brothers sat up drinking until 4 A.M. one morning.
By the end of the conversation Daniel had decided
to go along. In "The Trial of the Catonsville Nine,"
where Berrigan uses the court record as the basis
for a book suggested by the new theater of fact,
he includes lines from his testimony which describe that decision:

> *I saw suddenly and it struck*
> *with the force of lightning*
> *that my position was false*
> *I was threatened wih verbalizing*
> *my moral substance out of existence.*

Which is exactly how I felt about myself, and
most people I know in New York, while I was
talking with him.

It was only a few months ago, when Berrigan
was talking with some friends at Cornell about the
spring festival that would be held in his honor (of
which the freedom seder was the main event),
that he decided to defy arrest. He wanted "to re-
examine the whole concept of going to jail," he
says, and to see if it was possible to survive in an
underground, particularly an underground based
on nonviolence rather than bombing or the need
to ferry soldiers to Canada.

I wanted to confront the mythology of the

good guy whose goodness depends on his willingness to go to jail, the sort of idea that
spread with the civil rights movement and
Martin Luther King. All that's over now. The
important thing is to keep working.

This whole thing is really an experiment. Is
it historically ready? Can the resource of
community and shelter be devised, and not
just community and shelter but appropriate
action? I don't know. But certainly exploring
those questions through my actions makes
more sense than going through the unending
ritual of crime and punishment.

He constantly cautioned against describing his
activity in exaggerated rhetoric. "If you're going to
do something really different you must be careful
and thoughtful. So far we haven't really seen anything work in the movement. Not the draft-card
burnings, the massive mobilizations, the effort to
bring political changes. The movement has been
scattered without victories, the war effort has been
deflected into the environment. None of these
things has deepened the quality of our resistance
or changed our lives."

He did predict that new communities—"communes, really—will multiply rapidly and will be
increasingly responsible politically." Like the law
communes, they'll have roots in big cities so that
they are relevant to poor people and black people, he said. They will have to encourage the
crossing of generational and political lines. Thus,
professors will have to find a new way of relating
to students, perhaps living with students in communes, and start making trouble in departments
on their behalf, he continued. "These communes
should be encouraged wherever there are young
people and professionals, people who really want

to know if their lives are serving human needs."

But he didn't want me to imply that he had any kind of grand strategy. Nor was he sure of the relationship between the communes and the underground. "I'm almost Vietnamese in my sense of things. They've been fighting how long?—one thousand years, really—and they're still patient, still convinced they're right. To turn the United States around is a millennial project—if, of course, the United States doesn't destroy itself first. We have to concentrate on the quality of life, the creation of unusual human beings. There is no way to shorten a process which is bound to be long-term and bloody."

Then he praised the endurance of people like A. J. Muste and Dorothy Day, and said that the willingness to risk everything at one moment was useful only some of the time. There would have to be people whose dedication to working aboveground was just as intense as his dedication to working underground. "But one meets so many young people who want to risk their lives at one time and then, when little comes of a particular action, yield to drugs or despair and are never heard from again."

But were there groups as opposed to individuals in which he had confidence? As we continued to talk, I began to see the profound skepticism which underlies his belief that "to turn the United States around is a millennial project." The left, as he seems to see it, is almost as callow and greedy and violent as the society it seeks to change.

For example: "People in my own age group are paralyzed by a fear that they'll lose their income, their security. They'll march for anything. Nixon and Johnson appeal to a deep feeling in middle-aged Americans—a feeling that change comes with no loss except to the young, black, and poor."

The family, he said a little later, is "a sitting duck before the war machine. Its needs keep magnifying and it supports the system as consumers. The middle-class breeds kids to become social engineers, the poor breed kids to kill—and their progeny stays in conflict with each other and supports the state.

"Besides, there can't be one resisting member, one person underground, if the family wants to survive."

Then he described the kind of action the Weathermen have come to symbolize (he respected many of the individual Weathermen he knew at Cornell) as "the wildest kind of egotistical violence. That's the American character emerging."

What would alter that character? I asked.

"Well, very few of those people have had much experience outside their own culture. They haven't seen how America affects people elsewhere, or let themselves be broadened beyond the middle-class here."

Hesitantly, I asked him about the Committee of Returned Volunteers, whose members feel that we've been made more sensitive to the United States and its effects on other cultures by our Peace Corps stints overseas. But Berrigan was quite angry at C.R.V. He had met with some up-state New York chapters before going underground, and apparently they'd failed to respond to some requests he made. "They might call themselves radicals, but to me they seem eager to stay in graduate schools and earn their professional credentials. They want change without loss, too."

That is much less true than Berrigan thought

when we talked, before the invasion of Cambodia and the murders at Kent State. Last Friday a group of returned volunteers occupied the East Asia Wing of the Peace Corps building and held it through Saturday's demonstration, turning the street below into a liberated zone where people could rap with each other or dance or sleep. We weren't arrested, but that had been impossible to predict: we were prepared to go to jail when we entered the building.

Still, Berrigan's words struck a chord in me that afternoon. As I thought about them, I realized that the importance of cross-cultural experiences, even successful ones, is usually over-rated. They free you from the assumptions of the society where you were born, it's true, and leave you feeling home-less: many returned volunteers I know feel like foreigners here even after they've been back in the country for three or four years. But cross-cultural experiences cannot furnish the thing so many white Americans lack: a personal feeling for what it's like to be devastated, to lose everything through war or conquest. It's a sense of life's tragedy that Europeans possess because of the two great wars on their continent, that Asians, Africans, and Latin Americans possess because of their history of op-pression. But the illusion that our affluence is per-manent, willed by God, and the myth of our un-defeated, untied, unscored upon football record that Coach Nixon urged us to preserve in his locker-room speech on Cambodia has made most of us criminally careless about the consequences of our words and actions.

Now America is paying for that innocence with the civil war that escalated last week.

But who, I wondered, did Berrigan expect to

build the underground and the communes? He had
written off his contemporaries, families, my contemporaries who hadn't served abroad, my contemporaries who had served abroad. Where would
the "unusual humans" he had talked about earlier
come from?

"You have to remember that we're at a pre-
stage," he said; unusual humans were "those who
are willing to sit down and share their lives with
you. And I hope that such people will not see me
as an icon, but regard what I'm doing as an invitation to do the same."

As it had all afternoon, his emphasis on patience
made me doubt the American impulsiveness that I
never seem able to lose. I'd been talking, for example, about the need to control some land, perhaps even part of a state, where radicals could
begin to create humane institutions with which
people who consider themselves closer to the movement than to Nixonia could identify: a zone that
would serve the same sort of function as the Sierra
Maestras served in pre-revolutionary Cuba. Berrigan seemed interested, but I was sure that he considered my words a little rash and callow. I was
still operating within the Western political traditions which he wanted to transcend, still talking
about land and constituencies, power and major-
ities.

Berrigan had the modesty of most genuinely
courageous men and women: because he was certain of his ability to act according to his principles,
he didn't have to comfort himself with exaggerated
rhetoric or strategies. I'd been hoping that his
words would afford me some guidance for what
to do next, how to keep fighting through this
nightmare in which we're living now and still

sustain my faith in a more humane future. But he showed me that that knowledge would have to come from inside myself. . . . The readiness to act bravely releases one's imagination and sympathies as nothing else can.

Berrigan was talking about faith. He became most emotional when he described the possible meaning of his act for Catholics. "There might still be something to this faith, though not this religion. Jesus still means something to young people." Here his voice lilted and soared, he chuckled happily. "It's clear that He means something to young people.

"I turn my back on Cardinal Cooke's visits to the troops, but I stay with the life and death of Jesus."

Then he began to talk about Jesus's belief in nonviolence—and, I think, about the hope that undergirds his own act.

"Jesus decided in his own life that it was more important to undergo violence than to inflict it. He wasn't just offering that as one man's opinion. The Sermon on the Mount was a blueprint. It helps show how to look for the points of resistance that have to do with vindicating the dignity of man."

Four Sketches by People Who
   Sheltered Him

Dan Berrigan
with Families
in the
Underground

---

*The following is written by members of various
families with whom Daniel Berrigan stayed while
underground in the summer of 1970. These are impressions and notes; they are not meant to be representative of Father Berrigan's experience, or of
the experience of those people with whom he
stayed.*

I

When Dan was underground, it was no simple
matter for him to make a phone call. We all had
to develop a certain sensitivity to the government's
electronic surveillance network. "Safe" phones had
to be found, timing at both ends of the conversation had to be carefully arranged. For several days
Dan had been in the process of arranging such a
conversation with someone particularly dear to
him.

I was to drive him to a telephone, and as the
time for the call approached we both grew tense.
The easy ways we had with each other were lost
when it came time to leave the relative safety of

our home. Outside, where other people moved with impunity, every stop at a traffic light was a menace to us. Because we regarded our government as criminal, and our government regarded Dan and his friends as criminal, we and the government understood each other too well. When I stepped with Dan into the street I felt directly the guilt and terror and madness of America waging war. Fugitives see clearly.

We had chosen a public phone in a large busy shopping center. There was a row of glassed-in booths outside along the front of an enormous department store. We circled past the booths once to be sure there was nothing unusual. I felt Dan was eager to make this call, though he seldom showed strong feelings openly. I parked about twenty-five yards from the phone booth and stayed in the car while Dan walked across the crowded lot.

Once he was in the booth I tried to stay alert to the risks of his being recognized. A woman stepped into the booth beside him, but though they looked at each other through the glass, she didn't recognize him. She seemed to see nothing, her arms heavy with bundles, her mind with the weight of consuming. Dan seemed protected by the neon anonymity of the place. A police car cruised slowly past him, but the local police weren't likely to be looking for underground fugitives. They were there to protect the shopping center, to keep the conveyer belts rolling and the cash registers tallying. What was menacing the shopping center wasn't clear, unless it was that slender man bent earnestly toward a telephone who was asking Americans to stop consuming one another and the world.

For a moment with Dan there in the phone

booth, I saw that shopping center as the real state of the nation, its image reproduced a thousand-fold across the American landscape. A thick haze of artificial light overhead, food deceptively pack-aged and dangerously processed, people cramming their carts with goods, transacting faceless busi-ness, dressed in plastics, spraying plastics on their hair, striving to resemble department-store mani-kins that are the last sex gods and goddesses Americans will adore with the smell of popcorn in their nostrils. This was the consumer society. And yet I had come to shop here, and undoubtedly would come again. It was cheaper . . . it was that way with Dan: I saw things not bigger than life, but as they really were.

He came back from the phone booth smiling, moving quickly through the crowd. I assumed it had been a good conversation and his spirits were up. "No answer," he said. "There was no one there." There was no sadness or disappointment in his voice. "Maybe next time," he said, though we could have no idea when next time would be. Dan loved those people and it must have hurt him that the call hadn't gone through, but it seemed as though he had already converted his feelings into another kind of energy, another hope. He was smiling and looking with some bewilderment at the shopping center as we drove away.

II

One hot afternoon we decided without much pre-meditation to drive out to an ocean beach. We always tried to think through very carefully any plan that involved Dan's moving from place to place, and I stood there in the sun lamely trying to justify the risk, but Dan liked to celebrate and asked no more occasion than the heat of day.

We took off with no more precaution than a pair of sunglasses. It was a real outing, the children joyous with the suddenness of the thing (they hadn't even *asked* to go), and we older heads exhilarated by the chance to defy the government by taking to the beaches. Our only provisions were sandwiches for the kids, a bottle of Suoave Bolla chilling in a pail of ice, and a black pot full of steaming clams. It was our clear intention to build a fire at the beach and devour the tasty little marvels.

As we came closer to the crowded beach, we grew more apprehensive, and I mumbled that maybe we had been a little reckless. The children asked why we didn't just stop and pile out. "We're looking for the nicest place," I said, and kept driving until we found a fairly open stretch of beach.

Our children raced for the water, trailing sandpails and strainers and inner tubes. My wife and I were making cautionary glances left and right, but Dan had already stripped down to a baggy borrowed bathing suit and chased after the kids, running into the cold water without breaking stride. They played together in the surf, children and man, and we began to get some idea what we were celebrating.

Dan was the firebuilder. He showed the children what kind of driftwood to look for along the high-tide lines and we worked together until we had gathered enough to make a blaze. We dug out a pit in the sand and Dan stacked the wood carefully and then lit it, fanning the flames and study-

ing them with a strange concentration. I noticed
that the children were watching the fire with the
same rapt expression. But for Dan there was Catonsville in those flames, and a boy who had im-
molated himself outside a cathedral to express his
final outrage with the war, and David Darst burned
to death in a car crash, and Vietnam, and perhaps
purification.

We steamed those clams without remorse, and
feasted together, and drank off that fine bottle of
wine. Then we rested, watching the tide going out,
bathers slowly leaving and clam diggers coming,
and the sun setting behind us, deepening the
colors of the sky.

III

We had spoken before about choice and life
commitments. We were a "Movement family," all
of us veterans of demonstrations, teach-ins, sanctuaries. We had sat-in at draft boards, attended
trials, organized fund-raising events for resistance
groups and similar causes and we had taken part
in endless meetings. But somehow, when Dan came
into our midst, we were compelled to review our
lives from a new perspective. What did our convictions mean when weighed in terms of sacrifice and
risk? What were our responsibilities? And, regardless of our own beliefs, did we have the right to
jeopardize the safety and security of our children?

Having no immediately useful skills, legal, medical, technical, or even ideological, we had nothing
to offer—except our bodies and our lives. And we
had been raised according to the doctrines of
middle-class America. We were educated citizens

to whom time and knowledge were the currency of exchange. We served a valuable function just by perpetuating our sheer existence.

And here now—there entered into our lives a man who challenged all that—a man who, at evident cost to himself, had abandoned those things to which we clung—family, social position, the satisfaction of a career well carried out. But Dan was neither a monastic nor a nay-sayer. For him there was to be no rejection of family, of God, of Church, of Order, nor most significantly, of Country. He was devoted to them all. He loved people and he loved life.

His presence challenged us to reflect upon his life and upon our own. While we did worry over his safety and how to preserve it without creating a prison of our own, we probably expended more energy upon these deeper preoccupations that transcended the concerns of every day.

We had experienced very little hesitation in inviting Dan into our home. If anything, we were honored by the trust placed in us, and perhaps a little exhilarated by the mystery and romance of it all. But as the days passed, we found that Dan became a real and personal presence in our lives, a beloved friend, and a special guest.

At Dan's instigation we gathered together a small group of good and trusted friends, all like ourselves, settled people with children and responsibilities; and we spent a weekend at a country retreat. The purpose of our meeting was to consider how we and others like us could play a part in creating a new society—one which would be free of war and exploitation, of racism, and of the systematic dehumanization of persons to which we knew that the routine of our lives contributed.

Dan had a vision that in an atmosphere of retreat from the world, into ourselves, we would awaken to a new life and new possibilities. We would recognize the risks before us but look beyond them to new hope and new objectives, and we would find the strength and the will to move toward their achievement.

But it was not to be. Perhaps it was a sociological misjudgment on his part—perhaps a deficiency of dramatic and historical conversions. The mundane and the trivial prevailed—domestic chores to be done, children's needs to be attended, family squabbles and problems of discipline, noise, confusion, and moments of irritation and embarrassment. As we sat at the dinner table, we could not dispel annoyance at the whining mosquitoes and the importunate shufflings and yappings of family dogs exploring a new environment. Throughout the day, our conversations were interrupted by the tedious demands of children, children who, because they were ours and we loved them, could not be turned away. There was no peace for ideological contemplation, no atmosphere for mystical transformation—only the steady coerciveness of bourgeois life and our own reflection of bourgeois values.

Dan's self-restraint became increasingly visible. This was not what he had had in mind; and we, sensing his disapproval, withered in his gaze. All of us were accustomed to responding to challenge with guilt, to living with and loathing our own sense of inadequacy, and to the litany of self-accusation which among us substitutes for failure since we were—none of us—failures.

But was it wrong to be as we were, to love our children, to carry out our jobs, to be well-meaning, if somewhat uncomfortable people? Could we be expected to transform ourselves upon the instant and according to Dan's vision? He had wanted to bring us together as families, not young, not free, not unattached. And that is what we were—middle-class, liberal, and intellectual families predominantly Jewish. We did not share his heritage or his life style. Could we share his values? And if we could not, could we bear his disapproval? We reacted with fear and self-doubt.

Throughout one hot afternoon the tension mounted. The children became (or appeared to become) more shrill and demanding. Tempers were short and the air was heavy. We sat on the front porch talking about our lives, our professional commitments, and the sacrifices and compromises that we would and would not make. Dan was sitting to the side and slightly behind me. He was very silent, tipped back in his chair, a blade of grass between his teeth, and a frown upon his face. At that moment I did not like him.

Suddenly it came upon me that my resentment of him was not because of the disruption that he was causing in my life. In fact, I welcomed that. Rather, it was that all of us were laboring under misapprehensions, Dan as well as the rest of us. It was *wrong* for him to pretend to be, or for us to accept him as, our spiritual guide. He had no pastoral duties toward us and we could not be his flock. We had no obligation to satisfy *his* expectations, and no business making our desire to do so a primary concern—and he had no business demanding it. We did have an obligation to come to terms with our own lives, but those lives were and had to be independent of him. We had been seduced by the man and by our own romanticism to frame our lives in false images. It was with respect to our own integrity that we had to act, and not out of fear of his displeasure.

But it was with fear that I spoke. Was I hiding behind long-term commitments to return to a life of provincial self-absorption? Was this cowardice? lack of enterprise? selfishness or stagnation? Was I turning my back on the chance of a lifetime? I did not know what was right, but I did know that what was happening was wrong and that whatever we did had to be right for us, and not for someone else, however noble and lovable he might be. That is what I said, and at first there was anger—some moments of silent, subtle and guarded hostility. Conversations became disjointed. Eyes wandered and hands and feet moved restlessly. I felt a terrible flood of shame and sorrow. It was all over. I had spoiled our moment of greatness, and I wanted nothing so much as to get away—alone.

Solitude, however, is hard to come by and would have provided no escape. In fact the episode did not end so tragically or so dramatically, but rather inconclusively, and yet, I think, affirmatively. We met again in the evening, having swum and walked and reflected. We spoke matter of factly about concrete things, but in an atmosphere of respect and mutual understanding.

For myself, I know that I will not walk away from the life and the commitments I have made. But that life has a new quality; for I cannot return to it uncritically or unquestioningly. It will not remain unchanged. I am grateful to Dan and I love him for what he is, but I no longer fear his anger and disappointment, as I did. What is more, I have faith in him that he has faith in me, because that is his strength and his gift.

Shortly after the weekend Dan moved on and not much later was apprehended. I do not know what his recollection of that meeting might be, whether it was for him, as for me, charged with self-discovery, with fellow feeling, and with the joyful precariousness of human interchange. Perhaps it was just another retreat with the usual round of successes and disappointments, a few pleasant hours spent and an assortment of annoyances endured. I like to think that it meant more than that. But whatever it meant, I know that without the slightest hesitation I would do it again.

IV

Our youngest child awoke this morning saying, "I've dreamed of Dan." The dream was not fanciful but rather ordinary—Dan and our cat, Dan in the garden "making land," Dan looking at our new red floor. The child was radiant as he told this dream. There have been other times too since Dan was with us that the intensity of those few days seemed to return sharply. He heard Dan's voice (a record of his poems) and stood transfixed, afterward repeating Dan's words without understanding them, "I saw my sweet skin was hiding out behind others." And once I overheard the children confide to each other tolerantly that they understood Dan even if *he* didn't know the right word. "We knew he was trying to say tummy." Dan used to say "Gummy" as he tickled their ribs.

I think for instance of baking a pie with Dan, the children climbing about, wanting to help, my wanting to listen to Dan. We were talking about the pie and about family. The pie was a pecan pie which Dan had last made when he and Phil and Jerry were together. It was a revelation to me to sense, as he described the celebration that was their last evening together, the closeness of these brothers. I'd thought it was perhaps easy for a priest to be separate from friends and family. Dan is celibate and I'd thought these decisions of his made him different from us. It was only convenient and comfortable to think so. He had chosen a kind of freedom that allowed him to act out what he believed. Could we, our family, ever create such a freedom for ourselves?

Pecan shells on the floor, the syrup bubbling, children clamoring for their own turn to stir the pot and I handing them the spoon. Noticing that Dan hadn't my skill of tuning out the shrill intrusion of children's voices, I sent the children out. I stared momentarily out into the yard after them regarding them a bit angrily for their intrusion in our conversation. Dan had retreated and read the news and I was left to dwell on the brothers' situation. (Phil in prison, in solitary, held, as it were, hostage for Dan and yet Dan trusts completely that Phil is O.K., that to give himself up would be to give up the freedom that would be both of theirs as long as Dan remained at large in the underground.) When Dan re-enters the kitchen to check on his pies I glimpse a strange joy. He has just read that Phil is fasting to protest his own solitary and the greater mistreatment of other prisoners. That Phil is fasting seems to speak directly to Dan saying, yes, brother, this confinement, this fast is a cause for celebration.

The children are out and seem to be taking care

of each other. Because I am caught up in trying
to balance my time and all my concerns with their
needs I am intrigued to hear about Dan's mother,
who is the mother of six. He shares a letter with
me. She writes from the hospital wishing him well,
not knowing where he is or whether the letter will
reach him. She had not expected him to emerge
from the underground and visit her in the hospital,
but the F.B.I. had and had surrounded her with
its "extra protection."

And what if I should feel compelled to resist
the war as directly as Dan had? I felt at that moment so far from this grand old woman's depth of
understanding and from Dan's particular freedom
that had the children not rushed back in Dan might
have detected the effect his presence and sharing
this letter had on me. The children came laughing
into the house, Dan tickling their "Gummies" one
by one.

I remember that Dan didn't eat any of the pie
that night. Maybe no one else noticed, but I was
puzzled. He never explained.

We've tried to tell the children since Dan's capture who he is and why he is in jail. The older
ones seem to understand. They don't talk about it
much or dream about it. But the youngest is still
confused. "Is Dan caught in the war with the
'war men,' or is he in jail?" Perhaps his confusion
is accurate.

Daniel Berrigan, S.J.

Letter
to
the
Weathermen

Dear Brothers and Sisters,

This is Dan Berrigan speaking. I want to say what a very deep sense of gratitude I have that the chance has come to speak to you across the underground. It's a great moment when I can rejoice in the fact that we can at last start setting up a dialogue that I hope will be a continuing thing through the smoke signals, all with a view to enlarging the circle of those who realize that the times demand not that we narrow our method of communication but that we actually enlarge it if anything new or anything better is going to emerge. I'm talking out of a set of rough notes and my idea was that I could not only discuss these ideas with you but possibly publish them.

The Cold-War alliance between politics, labor, and the military finds many Americans at the right end of the cornucopia. What has not yet risen in them is the question of whose blood is paying for all this, what families elsewhere are being blasted, what separation and agony and death are the other side of that coin of the realm—the connections are very hard to make, and very few come on them, and many can hardly imagine that all being right with America means that very much must go wrong elsewhere. How do we get such a message across to others? It seems to me that that is one way of putting the very substance of our task. Trying to keep connections, or to create new ones. It's a most difficult job, and in hours of depression it seems all but impossible to speak to Americans across the military and diplomatic and economic idiocies—and yet I think we have to carry our reflection further and realize that the difficulty of our task is the other side of the judgment Americans are constantly making about us. This determination to keep talking with all who seek a rightful place in the world or all who have not yet awakened to it, this, I think, is the revolution, and the United States perversely and negatively knows it, and this is why we are in trouble. And this is why we accept trouble, and ostracism and the fear of jail and of death, as the normal conditions under which decent men are called upon to function today.

Undoubtedly the F.B.I. comes after people like me with guns because deeper than their personal chagrin and their corporate machismo, which is a kind of debased esprit de corps since they always get their man, there was that threat that the Panthers and the Vietnamese had learned so well as a reality. The threat is a very simple one because we are making connections, political connections, religious and moral connections, connections with prisoners and Cubans and Vietnamese, and these connections are forbidden under the policies which J. Edgar Hoover is greatly skilled both in enacting and in enforcing. They know by now what we are about, they know we are serious. And they are serious about us. Just as with a mortal fear for the

last five years they have known what the Vietnamese are about and the Brazilians and the An-
golese and the Guatemalans. We are guilty of
making connections, of urging others to explore
new ways of getting connected, of getting married,
of educating children, of sharing goods and skills,
of being religious, of being human, of resisting. I
am speaking for prisoners and exiles and that true
silent, deathly silent majority which is that of the
dead and the unavenged as well as the unborn,
and I am guilty again of making connections with
you.

By and large the public is petrified of you. There
is a great mythology surrounding you—much more
than around me. You come through in public as
another embodiment of the public nightmare which
is menacing and sinister and senseless and violent:
a spin-off of the public dread of Panthers and
Vietcong, of Latins and Africans, and the poor of
our country, of all those expendable and cluttering
and clamorous lives who have refused to lie down
and die on command or to perish at peace with
their fate, or to exist in the world as suppliants
and slaves.

But in a sense, of course, your case is even
more complicated because your choice to rebel is
not the passionate consequence of the stigma of
slavery. Yours is a choice. It's one of the few
momentous choices in American history. Your no
could have been a yes, and the society realizes it
because you had everything going for you. Your
lives could have been posh and secure, but you
said no. And you said it, moreover, by attacking
the very properties you were supposed to have in-
herited, a very amazing kind of turnabout.

The society, I think, was traumatized. What to

do with Vietcong or Panthers had never been a
very complicated matter, after all. We jailed them
or shot them down or brought in the National
Guard. But what to do with you—this indeed was
one hell of a question. There was no blueprint
and no answer. And yet this question, too, was not
long in being answered, as we learned at Kent
State. That is to say, when property and the question of its survival come up close, the metaphor is
once more invariably military. It is lives that go
down. And now we know that even if those lives
are white and middle-class, they are going to be
in the same gun-sights.

The mythology of fear that surrounds you is
exactly what the society demands, as it demands
more and more mythology, more and more un-
reality to live by. But it also offers a very special
opportunity to break this myth that flourishes on
silence and ignorance and has you stereotyped as
mindless, indifferent to human life and death, determined to raise hell at any hour or place. We
have to deal with this as we go along; but from
where, from what sort of mentalities, what views
of one another and ourselves? Not from an opposite window of insanity or useless rage, but with
a new kind of anger which is both useful in communicating and imaginative and slow-burning to
fuel the long haul which is the definition of our
whole lives.

I'm trying to say that when people look about
them for lives to run with and when hopeless people look for hope, the gift we can offer others is
so simple a thing as hope. As they said about Che,
as they say about Jesus, some people, even to this
day, he gave up hope. So that my hope is that you
see your lives in somewhat this way, which is to

say I hope your lives are about something more than sabotage. I'm certain they are. I hope the sabotage question is tactical and peripheral. I hope indeed that you are remaining uneasy about its meaning and usefulness, and that you realize that the burning down of properties, whether Catonsville or in the case of Chase Manhattan or anywhere else, by no means guarantees a change of consciousness, the risk remaining always very great that sabotage will change people for the worse and harden them against further change.

I hope you see your lives as Che saw his, that is to say mainly as teachers of the people, conscious as we must be of the vast range of human life that still awaits liberation and education and consciousness. If I'm learning anything it is that nearly everyone is in need of this and therefore in need of us, whether or not they realize it. I think of all those who so easily dismiss and whose rage against us is an index of the blank pages of their real lives, those to whom no meaning or value has ever been attached by politicians or generals or churches or universities or indeed anyone, those whose sons fight the wars, those whose wages are drained away paying for the wars, those who are constantly mortgaged and indebted to the consumer system, and those closer to ourselves, among fellow students who are still enchanted by careerism and selfishness, those who are unaware that the human future must be created out of suffering and loss.

How shall we speak to our people, to the people everywhere? We must never refuse, in spite of their refusal of us, to call them our brothers. I must say to you as simply as I know how, if the people are not the main issue, there is simply no main issue and you and I are fooling ourselves

also, and the American fear and dread of change
has only transferred itself to a new setting.

This, I think, is where a sensible, humane movement operates on several levels at once if it is to
get anywhere. So it is saying communication yes,
organizing yes, community yes, sabotage yes—as a
tool. That is the conviction that took us where
we went. And it took us beyond, to this night. We
reasoned that the effect of our act could not be
to impede the war or much less to stop the war in
its tracks. God help us, if that had been our intention, we were certainly fools before the fact
and doubly fools after it, for in fact the war went
on. And still we undertook sabotage long before
any of you. It might be worthwhile just very quickly reflecting on some reasons why. We were trying first of all to say something about the per-
nicious effect of certain properties on the lives of
those who guarded them or died in consequence of
them. And we were determined to talk to as many
people as possible and as long as possible afterward, to interpret and to write, and through our
conduct, through the appeal, through questioning
ourselves again and again, finding out where we
were, where we were going, where people might
follow.

My hope is that affection and compassion and
nonviolence are now common resources once more
and that we can proceed on that assumption, the
assumption that the quality of life within our
communities is exactly what we have to offer. I
think a mistake in S.D.S.'s past was to kick out any
evidence of that as being weakening or reactionary or counterproductive. The mark of inhuman
treatment of humans is a mark that also hovers

over us. It is the mark of a beast, whether its insignia is the military or the movement.

No principle is worth the sacrifice of a single human being. That's a very hard statement. At various stages of the movement some have acted as if almost the opposite were true, in that we get purer and purer. More and more people have been kicked out for less and less reason. At one period of the past, way back, the result of such thinking was another of the religious wars, or wars of extinction. At another time it was Hitler; he wanted a ton of purity too. Still another is still with us in the war against the Panthers and the Vietnamese. I think I'm in the underground because I want part of none of these, whatever name they go by, whatever rhetoric they justify themselves with.

When madness is the acceptable public state of mind, we're all in danger, all in danger for under the heel of former masters as under the heel of new ones.

Some of your actions are going to involve inciting and conflict and trashing, and these actions are very difficult for thoughtful people. But I came upon a rule of thumb somewhere which might be of some help to us: do only that which one cannot not do. Maybe it isn't very helpful, and of course it's going to be applied differently by the Joint Chiefs of Staff and the underground group of sane men and women. In the former, hypocritical expressions of sympathy will always be sown along the path of the latest rampage. Such grief is like that of a mortician in a year of plague. But I think our realization is that a movement has historic meaning only insofar as it puts its gains to the side dictated by human dignity and the protection of life, even of the lives most unworthy of such respect. A revolution is interesting insofar as it avoids like the plague the plague it promised to heal. Ultimately if we want to define the plague as death, and I think that's a good definition, the healing will neither put people to death nor fill the prisons nor inhibit freedom nor brainwash nor torture its enemies nor be mendacious nor exploit anyone, whether women or children or blacks or the poor. It will have a certain respect for the power of the truth, which created the revolution in the first place.

We may take it, I think, as a simple rule of thumb that the revolution will be no better and no more truthful and no more populist and no more attractive than those who brought it into being. Which is to say we are not killers, as America would stigmatize us, and indeed as America perversely longs for us to be. We are something far different, we are teachers of the people who have come on a new vision of things. We struggle to embody that vision day after day, to make it a reality among those we live with so that the people are literally disarmed by knowing us, so that their fear of change, their dread of life is exorcised, and their dread of human differences is slowly expunged.

Instead of thinking of the underground as temporary or exotic or abnormal, perhaps we are being called upon to start thinking of its implication as an entirely self-sufficient, mobile, internal revival community, so that the underground may be the definition of our future. What does it mean literally to have nowhere to go in America or to be kicked out of America? It must mean to us— let us go somewhere in America, let us stay here and play here and love here and build here, and in this way join not only those who like us are recently kicked out also, but those who have never been inside at all, the blacks and the Indians and Puerto Ricans and Chicanos, whose consciousness has gone far under the rock.

Next, we are to strive to become such men and women as may, in a new world, be nonviolent. If there's any definition of the new man, the man of the future, it seems to me that we do violence unwillingly, bar exception, as instrument, knowing that destruction of property is only a means and keeping the end as vivid and urgent and as alive to us as are the means so that the means are judged in every instance by their relation to the ends. I have a great fear of American violence, not only out there in the military and the diplomacy, in economics, in industry and advertising, but also in here, in me, up close among us.

On the other hand, I must say, I have very little fear, from firsthand experience, of the violence of the Vietcong or Panthers (I hesitate to use the word violence), for their acts come from the proximate threat of extinction, from being invariably put on the line of self-defense, but that's not true of us and our history. We can simply say from outside the culture of these others, no matter what admiration or fraternity we feel, we are unlike them, we have other demons to battle.

But the history of the movement, in the last years, it seems to me, shows how constantly and easily we are seduced by violence, not only as to method but as to end in itself. With very little politics, very little ethics, very little direction, and only a minimum moral sense, if any at all, it might lead one to conclude in despair: the movement is debased beyond recognition, I can't be a part of it. Far from giving birth to the new man, it has only proliferated the armed, bellicose, and inflated spirit of the army, the plantation, the corporation, the diplomat.

Yet it seems to me good, in public as well as in our own house, to turn the question of violence back on the true creators and purveyors of it, working as we do from a very different ethos and for very different ends. I remember being on a television program recently and having the whole thing thrown at me, and saying—look, ask the question in the seats of power, don't ask it of me, don't ask me why I broke the law, go ask Nixon why he breaks the law constantly, ask the Justice Department, ask the racists. Obviously, but for Johnson and Nixon and their fetching ways, Catonsville would never have taken place and you and I would not be here today, just as but for the same people S.D.S. would never have grown into the Weathermen or the Weathermen have gone underground. In a decent society, normally functioning for its people, all of us would be doing the things that decent men do for one another. That we are forbidden so to act, forced to meet so secretly and with so few, is a tragedy we must live with. We have been forbidden a future by the forms of power, which include death as the ordinary social method, by having rejected the future they drafted us into and having refused, on the other hand, to be kicked out of America, either by aping their methods or leaving the country.

The question now is what can we create. I feel at your side across the miles, and I hope that sometime, sometime in this mad world, in this mad time, it will be possible for us to sit down face to face, brother to brother, sister to sister, and find that our hopes and our sweat, and the hopes and sweat and death and tears and blood of our brothers throughout the world, have brought to birth that for which we began.

Thank you and shalom.

Robert Coles

Thinking About Those Priests

As Philip Nobile has reported earlier in this volume, I was reluctant indeed to heed the request of some medical and divinity students that I visit Philip Berrigan in Lewisburg Prison. And I hesitated again when it was suggested to me that I meet with Daniel Berrigan and begin (perhaps) to tape record for publication some "conversations" which would presumably help clarify our various "positions" on any number of matters. I was honestly worried about my work, yet if anything (I now realize) the discussions about the Berrigan brothers that I eventually had with the mostly Catholic, so-called lower middle class families I work with have helped that work along considerably. I had feared that the two policemen and their families whom I visit, and the fireman, and the factory workers and white collar workers, would be made suspicious and angry were they to learn that I was visiting a man whose purposes and involvements I knew they distrusted. (I knew that there was no point in my going to Lewisburg if I could not make my observations public thereafter, if there were compelling reason to do so.) Instead I discovered that I had all along underestimated the men and women

I wanted so much to know—underestimated their complexity, the ambiguity of their thinking, the inconsistencies they (like all proud intellectuals) are capable of struggling with and even enjoying. I was told to go ahead and visit "the one in prison," and later I was told to go ahead and talk with "the one on the lam." (The two policemen I especially spoke to about my worries and hesitations could not for the life of them remember whether it was Phil or Dan who was already caught.)

Of course I was told other things, too. I was told that the Berrigans were foolish and no doubt being used by "clever Communist types." I was also told that there is a lot of injustice in this world, some of it so awful that "maybe we need a few priests who take on everyone, from the President down." Finally (and ironically) I was told to "go help them—*save* them." The man who said that was not being funny, and I quote him not to be funny myself by using him in a condescending manner. Nor were my capacities being overestimated. Here is the immediate context of the suggestion: "Don't you think they've got themselves into a terrible situation, the two of them? They've got the whole United States government against them, and I'm not sure they've accomplished a single thing. I'm a policeman. I think about all of this a lot: how far can you go if you think something is wrong, and no one is doing anything about it in City Hall or the State House or down there in Washington, D.C.? Those damn college students think they're the only ones who want this world to be a better place. My grandfather used to give me long sermons on the Yankees and the English, and how they own the banks and run the big universities and get their way all the time—in Ireland and here. Once I

asked him why he and my father and my uncles
and all our neighbors don't just start marching
and take over some of the banks. (It was the
depression, and we were in bad shape, real bad
shape.) I said we had relatives on the police, and
plenty of friends on the force, too. So they'd help
us, I was sure.

"My grandfather laughed, and so did my father
later on, when he heard what I'd said. My grandfather told me that people don't just go and do
or say what they think they should. He said
sometimes they're not sure what they should be
doing or saying, and sometimes they're just plain
scared. And I'll tell you, that's how I think today.
I guess most of us go along with the way things
are. It's beyond the ordinary man's imagination—
how to change things and make the country better
by evening things out, so there's not the very rich
and the very poor. And even if you can figure out
a way of making yourself heard, you've only got
this one life here on earth, and you have your
wife and kids, and you don't want to spend years
and years in prison, thinking how virtuous you
are. At least I don't. And besides, I do think in
this country there are changes taking place. Where
is there a better country?"

Then he went on to tell me that he was sure
the Berrigans were in more trouble than they had
bargained for; and he urged me to do what I
could to "straighten them out." He told me he
was sure *he* could, if somehow it were possible
for him and them to get together. He would tell
them what he told me, and perhaps they would
listen. The trouble with them, he believed, was
that up to now they have been "keeping the wrong
company" and been "egged on by people who aren't

footing the bill, people who are free while the two of them, priests mind you, are in prison."

I doubt that anything I say here or have already said on this vexing subject will be more significant than what that Boston policeman said to me in July of 1970. He knows (every day he is reminded) how complicated our society is—how much leeway we have, but also how limited our freedom is, and to a certain extent has to be. And he knows how frightened a big, burly man like himself, an *armed* man, can nevertheless feel day in and day out. I claim no less fear than he is willing to acknowledge—and I also feel deep within myself many of the attachments and loyalties and sentiments he conveys, given half a chance. (How many of us ever-so-articulate and self-assured teachers and students and doctors and lawyers have given him that chance, have tried to learn what he has to say, what he sees happening, what he lives through all the time as a man caught by his very occupation on the frontier of social unrest and change?) Certainly I disagree with him, too. We have argued many times. But I cannot believe that all of us who appear in this particular book, and many others who have responded to the call of the Berrigan brothers, do not feel at some critical point in our lives as troubled and confused as he does.

Yes, "liberals" like myself can make too much of that confusion—ours and everyone else's. We can argue ourselves and everyone else into inertia and apathy we perhaps all along find decisively reassuring. The longer we torment ourselves by weighing things and measuring things and skeptically analyzing things, the less likely it is that we will take a stand against anyone or anything very important or powerful. Still, I do not believe the

Berrigans did lightly what they did, and I do
not believe any of us has the right to decide for
the next man what his political position ought
to be. What we each of us have to do is settle for
ourselves where we stand—and hope we can be as
exemplary as possible in so doing. And here the
Berrigans have succeeded rather well; they have
pressed their ideals and deeds upon the policemen
I talk with and the students I teach at Harvard
and my colleagues in medicine and psychiatry—
to the point that none of us can be easily rid of
them. *"I was thinking about those priests,* just
thinking and thinking about them last night after
you left,"* I heard one morning from that same
policeman. He spoke emphatically, earnestly—and
surely he was responding to the intensity of the
conversation *we* had—he and I; but we have had
many vigorous and heated talks, none as hard for
him to put out of his mind. So much of what we
think about is necessarily concrete or (in the case
of people like me, but also people like that policeman) irresolvably unavoidably—or so it seems—
abstract. In the spring and summer of 1970 the
example of the Berrigans made it a little harder
for me to oscillate—even as the policeman does—
between the specific responsibilities I have to face
every day and the larger values I think about—
or often enough don't really think about at all,
just live by.

I hope some day the Berrigans will be able to
talk with these families I have talked with—talk
with them as openly and forcefully as they have
addressed other communities. I find it a tragedy
that the genuine populism, the real sense of fair
play, and not least, the deep religious faith I hear
expressed (or better, see manifested in such fami-

lies) is somehow cut off from others—from students who burn with anger at the injustices they feel they are alone in seeing in this world, from political activists who want to rally millions on behalf of one or another cause, yet can have such trouble reaching those who share neither the same vocabulary nor (often enough) the same assumptions. The last thing Dan Berrigan asked me—we had finished with the tape recorder, thank God—was about the people I seem so compelled to write about when I try to come to terms with what I think about him and his brother Phil. I told him how mixed my feelings are sometimes as I listen, for example, to the policeman I have quoted in this essay—and again, how mixed my feelings are when I listen to many speakers talk (and talk and talk) on university campuses. Rather obviously my feelings are mixed, period; but Dan did emphasize to me then, as we prepared to say goodbye (as he had on other occasions) the uncertainty he also felt. "We are groping," he said. Then he became a little stern and added: "We shouldn't be sure of ourselves, because we can't be, not now—not ever." I liked that—not only because I was gently let off a sort of hook, but because I really do believe there are many of us of all classes and backgrounds who have a lot to offer, as well as to teach, one another; and the last thing we ought to allow to happen is for that potential further to be diminished by those who won't for the life of them be caught groping: who will only be ever so sure of themselves.

The United States of America vs. The Berrigans: Some Documents

I

On Friday, November 27, 1970, J. Edgar Hoover, director of the F.B.I., appeared before a closed session of a Senate Appropriations subcommittee and made the sensational charge that the Berrigan brothers were leaders of a plot to blow up Washington power lines and kidnap a high White House official. Senator Robert C. Byrd (D., W. Va.), chairman of the subcommittee, said that he and Senator Roman L. Hruska (R., Neb.) were the only subcommittee members present, but did not think to request more details about the alleged plot. "I'd like to know who the White House official is," Senator Byrd said later. "I don't know why I didn't ask him." Hoover's remarks were subsequently released by the subcommittee in a transcript prepared by the F.B.I. Here are excerpts from those remarks:

Willingness to employ any type of terrorist tactics is becoming increasingly apparent among extremist elements. One example has recently come to light involving an incipient plot on the part of an anarchist group on the east coast, the so-called "East Coast Conspiracy to Save Lives."

This is a militant group, self-described as being composed of Catholic priests and nuns, teachers, students and former students who have manifested opposition to the war in Vietnam by acts of violence against Government agencies and private corporations engaged in work relating to U.S. participation in the Vietnam conflict.

The principal leaders of this group are Philip and Daniel Berrigan, Catholic priests who are currently incarcerated in the Federal Correctional Institution at Danbury, Connecticut, for their participation in the destruction of Selective Service records in Baltimore, Maryland, in 1968.

This group plans to blow up underground electrical conduits and steam pipes serving the Washington, D.C., area in order to disrupt Federal Government operations. The plotters are also concocting a scheme to kidnap a highly-placed Government official. The name of a White House staff member has been mentioned as a possible victim. If successful, the plotters would demand an end to United States bombing operations in Southeast Asia and the release of all political prisoners as ransom. Intensive investigation is being conducted concerning this matter.

II

On Saturday, November 28, in a statement released through two of their lawyers in New York, the Berrigans said:

On Friday, Mr. Hoover singled us out as leaders of an East Coast Conspiracy to Save Lives. We are happy to agree that such a conspiracy of conscience does exist, in a far more extensive form than Mr. Hoover recognizes. There is also a West Coast Conspiracy to Save Lives, a Middle Western Conspiracy to Save Lives, a Middle Atlantic and a Southern Conspiracy to Save Lives. There is, in fact, a Worldwide Conspiracy to Save Lives and "to demand an end to U.S. bombing operations in Southeast Asia."

Mr. Hoover, however, is overgenerous. At Danbury we have neither the facilities nor personnel to conduct such an enterprise. Nor do we have access to government funds. We have already been tried and condemned by Mr. Hoover's remarks, and we should have an equal opportunity to answer his charges. He ought, in view of the seriousness of the allegations he has made, either to prosecute us or publicly retract the charges he has made.

III

On Monday, November 30, Representative William R. Anderson (D., Tenn.), the Annapolis graduate, war hero, and one-time confirmed "hawk" on the Indochina war who had interested himself in the Berrigans after having read their writings on the war, wrote a letter to Mr. Hoover:

Since childhood, I have retained a great respect for the F.B.I. and its distinguished and dedicated Director. It is important for me to point that out so that you will realize that this letter is in no way an attack on you personally or on the vital agency you head.

This past Friday you were reported to have told a Senate Appropriations subcommittee that Fathers

Daniel and Philip Berrigan are the principal leaders of a plot to kidnap a White House staff member
in order to demand as ransom an end to U.S.
bombing operations in Southeast Asia and the release of political prisoners in the nation. You were
reported to have added that the group headed
by the Berrigans also planned to blow up underground electrical circuits and steam pipes in
Washington in order to disrupt operations of the
Federal Government.

I have become acquainted with the Berrigan
brothers through their writings and more recently
through three visits with them at the Danbury Federal Prison, the last of which was yesterday. As
you know, they are now serving sentences for vio-
lating the law by the destruction of draft records,
an act which I do not condone. This notwithstanding, it has become very apparent to me that Fathers Daniel and Philip Berrigan have something
from which we can all learn. Seldom do men of
such giant intellectual capacity come along. Even
more rarely do we see men so committed to the
poor, the oppressed, and the victims of war as to
purposefully risk imprisonment in order to project
and dramatize their beliefs.

The Berrigans have always followed a course
of total non-violence toward their fellow human
beings. To do otherwise would be to contradict
their fundamental beliefs. Thus it was quite a
shock for me to read of the very serious allegations
you have made against these men—allegations regarding their role in planning some very serious
crimes of violence.

If there is any substance to your allegations
against the Berrigans, Mr. Hoover, I respectfully
submit that it is your duty to arraign them before

a federal grand jury to seek an indictment. If, on the other hand, there is no substance, or if your remarks were misconstrued, then certainly we should expect an explanation, if not an outright retraction.

This matter goes beyond the Berrigan brothers in that unwittingly, I am sure, it adds to what seems to be a growing tendency on the part of our Executive Branch to employ the tactics of fear and to be less than candid in dealing with the public. I am sure, Sir, that you will agree that our system of government is endangered when anything less than an open, candid and humble relationship exists between the government and the people.

I will be anxious to hear from you on this matter.

On Wednesday, December 2, Mr. Hoover replied to Rep. Anderson:

I have received your letter of November 30, 1970, containing your observations regarding my testimony before the Senate Appropriations Subcommittee concerning Fathers Daniel and Philip Berrigan. I was surprised to observe that your letter was released to the press prior to its receipt by me.

You may be assured my testimony was predicated on the results of careful investigation. All information developed regarding this matter is being furnished to the Department of Justice, which has the responsibility for initiating prosecutive action.

IV

On Wednesday, December 9, Congressman Ander-
son took his case to the House Floor during special
orders. Excerpts from his remarks as reported in
the Congressional Record, 9 December 1970, Vol.
116, No. 197, pp. H11441-H11450:

Mr. Speaker:

Just recently there came to my attention some
very eloquent and meaningful words on the subject
of revolution:

". . . the truly revolutionary force of history is
not material power but the spirit of religion.
The world today needs a true revolution of the
fruitful spirit, not the futile sword. Hypocrisy,
dishonesty, hatred, all of these must be destroyed and men must rule by love, charity,
and mercy."

Are these the deeply reflective words of a cler-
gyman, a member of the anti-Vietnam war movement—perhaps Daniel or Philip Berrigan?

No, they are the inspiring words of F.B.I. Director J. Edgar Hoover. (*Masters of Deceit,* 1958.)

I'm sure the Reverend Father Philip Berrigan,
S.S.J., and his brother, the Reverend Daniel Berrigan, S.J., will agree with Mr. Hoover that man
"must rule by love, charity and mercy." But from
their cells in a federal penitentiary in Danbury,
Connecticut, it may be difficult for them to find
any love, mercy or charity in Mr. Hoover's charges
that they are the leaders of a kidnapping and
bombing plot.

These charges are of grave national importance
and America has been informed of them by the

news media—"bomb plotters . . . concocting a scheme to kidnap a highly placed government official . . ." If true, the Berrigans should be punished according to law, and they would expect this.

But any serious observer of this unpleasant episode in the life of the Berrigans—and this departure from due process by the director of the F.B.I. —need make only one conclusion: wars play strange tricks on many distinguished citizens.

The war—so appalling and tragic, so revolting and destructive—has forced Fathers Daniel and Philip Berrigan to climax a lifetime of service which includes in both instances service to the Armed Forces of the U.S., a lifetime of love and brotherhood, a lifetime of gentle persuasion against poverty and oppression, with the dramatic, illegal act of destroying draft records, a step which we the Members of the House cannot condone.

J. Edgar Hoover's actions seem likewise to be drastically affected by the tensions of this war. After a lifetime of dedicated service to the well-being of this nation—from gangbusting during prohibition, to protecting us from spies and espionage during war time—Mr. Hoover has resorted to tactics reminiscent of McCarthyism, using newspaper headlines and scare dramatics rather than the due process of law he has so proudly upheld in his distinguished career since he joined government service under President Calvin Coolidge.

We have suffered many casualties in the Vietnam War. Most of our domestic and international problems are either caused by this unwanted, undeclared war or are intensified by it.

It is now distressingly evident that one of the most ardent, devoted and, presumably, unassailable public servants in the lifetime of our Republic is, in a sense, a casualty of that same war.

As a lifelong admirer of Mr. Hoover and the F.B.I., I am convinced that he would not purposely subvert the Constitution or undermine our democratic processes. Yet it is manifest that on Friday, November 27, 1970, he did so. The divisions within our nation, the fear and repression so common in today's society have taken, we must conclude, another victim—the sense of fairness, the honorable ethics of justice that the FBI director has always held so high. . . .

HOOVER'S ALLEGATIONS IMPOSSIBLE TO BELIEVE

Knowing the Berrigan brothers and being reasonably well acquainted with their careers as priests, theologians, scholars and their dedication to Christian principles, and having read much of their writings, I found it impossible to believe that Mr. Hoover's allegations are true. Even in destroying draft files, illegal acts which they committed to dramatize the death toll of young American boys in Vietnam, they were meticulously careful to plan the events so that no physical harm could possibly befall clerks, bystanders, police or anyone else. The high crimes Mr. Hoover accused them of plotting would involve violence and pose threats to human welfare and possibly human life, which are actions that contradict the nonviolent life style of these Catholic priests.

Even if Mr. Hoover's allegations are based on substance, presuming he has hard evidence, why did he depart so radically from his charter and his own cherished, highly publicized tradition of seeking justice by due process. To use his words, "In the F.B.I. our objective is to secure the facts. We do not evaluate. The F.B.I. is strictly a fact-gathering agency responsible in turn to the Attorney General, the President, the Congress and in the last analysis to the American people."

We must ask why has Mr. Hoover departed so radically from established procedure by making such damaging charges in newspaper headlines which deny the Berrigan brothers an opportunity to meet their accuser in court. Why, we must ask, has Mr. Hoover broadcast these allegations, using the United States Senate as a forum instead of presenting the facts to the Justice Department, who would then, in due process, analyze them and, if warranted, present them to a federal grand jury? Mr. Hoover, a champion of law and order, has moved a step away from justice—by ignoring the system he recommends so highly to the opponents of this war. Surely his actions cannot help but contribute to the credibility gap many young Americans feel exists in our system of law and justice.

There are other questions. Is our Federal Bureau of Prisons so lax in its procedures that inmates can effectively plot and lead such high crimes? Is the director of the F.B.I. pointing the finger of scorn and malpractice at the Justice Department which administers the F.B.I. and the Federal Bureau of Prisons?

Then there is the all-important question of those constitutional rights protected by the First Amendment. The Berrigans are unable to speak out publicly, unable to respond personally to the questions of the press. Thus far they have been denied that cherished American right of facing their accuser.

Yet these allegations of bombings and kidnappings will be damaging and derogatory information available to parole boards who will later evaluate their "rehabilitation."

In 1954, writing in *American Magazine*, Mr. Hoover stated, "False accusations and careless insinuations can do more to destroy our way of life than to preserve it."

If Mr. Hoover's charges against the Berrigans of bomb and kidnapping plots are of this nature, Mr. Hoover can vindicate himself by an apology. If they are not false or careless, then we have a right to expect the Justice Department to institute federal grand jury proceedings promptly. Barring one of the two, we can only conclude that Director Hoover is unwittingly, I surely hope, involved in a process destructive of the institution he has loved and served with such loyal dedication. If his actions stem from such a degree of rage or fear that his purpose is to discredit all who peaceably and without violence oppose the Vietnam war, then I must again conclude, with much sadness, that he, too, is a victim of that war. . . .

CIVIL WAR IN AMERICA TODAY

In the course of the last thirty years, either as a member of the armed forces or as a member of the House of Representatives, I have participated, in combat and in debate, in the complex issues of peace and war. I have been a student of war. Now I want to balance the study of war with the study of peace.

My career in military or congressional service has been guided by the basic oath of office which obligates me to "protect and preserve the Constitution of the United Sates of America." It is the performance of this sworn duty that I speak.

The power to destroy civilization, as we know civilization, is available to several powers on earth, including the United States. We can, by default or by deliberate action, bring forth a havoc by weaponry that could reduce mankind to a primitive state.

America is now in its thirtieth year of war—cold or hot—thirty years of war that has seen more than a trillion dollars invested in refining the art of destruction . . .

America is in the midst of another civil war, a psychological civil war. Our youth are divided against themselves. Some join the military, accepting it as a citizen's duty; others reject the military service of destruction, reminding us in Congress that there is another war going on at home and around the world—a war that has a higher moral purpose, a higher ethical and spiritual involvement —the war against poverty, the war for better schools, housing, hospitals, the war in which the weapons are not the hardware of destruction, but the software of brotherhood and love. The technology is not militaristic, but humanistic, against disease and despair.

One war has brute killing as an objective, the other reveres living in freedom and justice as a fulfillable promise of life.

America is divided at the crossroads. Its heritage challenged.

In this confused environment, Congress has an obligation to listen to all voices, all points of view. Congress must homogenize the harsh voice with the soft voice. We must modify the tensions of the moment with the wisdom accumulated in history, and anticipate a future that rejects militarism as the only solution to mankind's conflicts.

During recent months this nation has witnessed a growing tendency on the part of our executive branch to employ the tactics of fear and to be less than candid in dealing with the public.

America's dilemma involves the negativism of the Indochina war versus the positive needs of our domestic realities. One asset is free discussion, the right of a free people peaceably to petition its government without harassment or the stifling of legitimate debate, proper and legal protest, and honest dissent.

Father Philip Berrigan, S.S.J., and Father Daniel Berrigan, S.J., have been convicted of destroying draft records. They make no protest of innocence. Indeed, they remain proud that their act of destruction against paper files symbolically represents an act to save the lives of young American soldiers—and save, too, the lives of the Vietnamese people, our allies, or the victims of our weapons.

HARASSMENT OF FR. PHILIP BERRIGAN

The verbal assault by Mr. Hoover on Fathers Berrigan is the climax of a series of events during the past several months which, when taken as separate incidents, are shocking and unbelievable, but when related one to the other, emerge as an outrageous pattern of fear and repression.

It is the common practice of the Bureau of Federal Prisons to assign political prisoners who have no previous pattern of common criminality to minimum security situations, usually a prison farm or similar institution. Despite this long-established procedure, Father Philip Berrigan was assigned to Lewisburg Penitentiary, a facility with tight security.

While there he was committed to solitary confinement situations for such minor infractions of prison regulations as offering spiritual counsel to a fellow prisoner and seeking opportunities to perform religious services. His fasting for ten days in protest of his solitary confinement led to the discontinuation of these practices.

Although Father Philip Berrigan was not assigned to a minimal security farm institution, he was returned to the general prison population at Lewisburg Penitentiary. During the confinement of Father Philip Berrigan before his brother was captured, he claims he was offered various inducements if he aided in the apprehension of his brother, and, conversely, he was subjected to threats of loss of privileges if he declined to aid the Justice Department's efforts to capture the elusive member of the Society of Jesus.

We should seriously examine the charge that privileges can be extended or denied, depending on the prisoner's willingness to cooperate with the F.B.I. and other Justice Department agencies.

Later, after the capture of Father Daniel Berrigan, both brothers were assigned to the minimum security prison at Danbury, where they remain, at this date, in custody.

During the indoctrination process, prison officials, with a pride that is difficult to justify, described a factory in the Danbury installation making weapon component parts for the Defense Department. The prisoners are paid, depending on skills and other considerations, wages that vary between 17¢ an hour and 46¢ an hour. Both Berrigans indicated that

they could not, as a matter of conscience, participate in this war industry work. The prison officials
did not press the issue.

High prison officials boasted, however, that the
Federal Bureau of Prisons made an annual profit
of $6,000,000 in this or other production facili-
ties . . .

Certainly prison employment is desired, but is it
necessary to use war-related enterprises as part of
the training programs in the federal prison system?

One other interesting characteristic of our federal
prison system has been brought to my attention by
Fathers Philip and Daniel Berrigan.

At Danbury, supervisory and management personnel—perhaps as many as twelve—are employed
to supervise the manufacturing facility. But only
one psychiatrist is employed. The present doctor is
accepting his service in the federal prison as
an alternate to military service. I have every reason
to believe the doctor is a competent, dedicated
practitioner. But it seems worthy of investigation
that funds are available for professional manufacturing personnel at a prison factory at salaries
competitive to private industry, but professional
psychiatric service is restricted to one man doing
alternate military duty.

Although the Berrigan brothers have been confined to Danbury federal prison for only four
months, they have spoken to me of other incidents
which contribute to a pattern of harassment by the
Justice Department.

HARASSMENT OF FR. DANIEL BERRIGAN

A court in Rochester, New York, required the
appearance of Father Daniel Berrigan, S.J., as a

witness in a matter unrelated to him. This writ was served on prison officials.

This was his experience:

On a late afternoon, Father Berrigan was advised to "get ready, you're being moved."

The prison officials would not inform him of where he was going, why, or under what authority. They did not show him or tell him about the court order. He was not permitted to advise his attorneys or his family. He was transferred from prison to prison, and ultimately to a county jail, never knowing his destination, never being advised of the court order, never having access to attorneys or family. At all times he was isolated in solitary confinement in the prisons or jail in which he was being kept.

But the strangest part of this odyssey of the Jesuit in custody of the Department of Justice is this: while being transported between county jail, prisons and court, Daniel Berrigan was secured with leg shackles, and waist chains to which his handcuffed wrists were locked in such a manner that he could not even use his handkerchief.

One prisoner, a priest, in the custody of three federal marshals, all armed, hardly needs leg irons, waist chains and handcuffs. The last time I saw leg shackles was in Con Son Island prison camp, in the tiger cages of the South Vietnamese government.

Father Daniel Berrigan, however, assured me that no one threw lime in his eyes, and asked that any plea related to the treatment he received be addressed not to his case, but in behalf of all prisoners.

It is fundamental in American heritage that all Americans can practice their religious freedoms. Indeed, in prison, criminologists agree that spiritual exercises, counseling and services are a beneficial part of the rehabilitative process. As a matter of record, this House approves appropriations for various agencies of the Justice Department which includes salaries for chaplains in prisons throughout the federal system.

The Berrigans' religious experiences in prison have been demeaning and rude.

It must be remembered that, although these men can be described in civil language as convicted felons, they are now and have been for the major part of their mature life distinguished theologians, respected by religious leaders of all denominations the world over for their commitment and dedication to the poor and oppressed, for their leadership in concepts of love, brotherhood, justice, compassion and for an activist life in the service of their true Master.

They are now, despite their custody in a federal prison, and have always been, in good standing with all faculties, rights and privileges implied in their ordination to their priesthood.

If their superiors in their church continue to accept them as priests of God, the Justice Department does not. If their religious orders—the Society of St. Joseph (S.S.J.) and the Society of Jesus (S.J.)—accept their interpretations of Gospel truths, the prison system fears them.

Yet at Danbury federal prison these two priests are not permitted to say Mass with voluntary attendance by other prisoners and guards. The Bureau of Federal Prisons refuses this religious request, despite the advantages potential to rehabilitation.

What is the reason for denying the simple right to celebrate Mass and preach the fundamental word of God's gospel? Is it a fear that the Berrigans might influence other prisoners with their message of peace, their message of brotherly love in prison?

Aristotle, nearly 2,000 years ago, identified the Berrigans' plight of denied spiritual exercises: *"The generality of men are naturally apt to be swayed by fear—rather than by an almighty reverence."*

Thus we see a connective pattern emerging—a pattern so compacted in only four months in prison that one must conclude the presence, in the Justice Department, of a tolerant attitude toward repressive harassment. These events are hardly coincidental.

Either the Berrigans, charged with bomb plots and kidnapping schemes, are dangerous—or there is a still more dangerous plot afoot to repress their political dissent against war and injustice.

V

On Thursday, December 10, President Nixon held his first nationally televised news conference in some months. Dan Rather, White House correspondent for CBS News, asked him if he approved of J. Edgar Hoover's recent actions. Nixon ignored all but one part of the question. The full text of Rather's question and Nixon's answer:

Q. Mr. President, as a lawyer and as his immediate superior, do you approve of the following actions of F.B.I. Director J. Edgar Hoover? One accusation which has been made public—accusing two men of conspiring to kidnap Government officials and/or blow up Government buildings as an antiwar action before any formal charges had been made and a trial could be arranged for those gentlemen. And continuing to call the late Martin

Luther King a liar. Do you approve of those actions?

A. I have often been asked about my opinion of Mr. Hoover. I believe that he has rendered very great service to this country. I generally approve of the action that he has taken. I'm not going to go into any of the specific actions that you may be asking about tonight with regard to the testimony, for example, that you referred to. The Justice Department is looking into that testimony that Mr. Hoover has given and will take appropriate action if the facts justify it.

VI

On Tuesday, January 12, 1971, Attorney General John Mitchell announced that a Federal grand jury in Harrisburg, Pa., indicted Fr. Philip Berrigan and five others on Federal charges of plotting to kidnap Henry Kissinger, assistant to the President for national security affairs, and to blow up the heating systems of Federal buildings in Washington. Seven others, including Fr. Dan Berrigan, were named in the indictment as co-conspirators but not as defendants.

Comment by Rep. Anderson: "I am delighted that the matter has finally been removed from the trial-by-headline arena. At last the matter is in proper judicial channels."

The
Indictment

**UNITED STATES DISTRICT COURT FOR THE
MIDDLE DISTRICT OF PENNSYLVANIA**

UNITED STATES
OF AMERICA,

        Plaintiff,

              Indictment No. : 14886

      v.   Violations   : 18 U.S.C. 371

                          18 U.S.C. 1201

EQBAL AHMAD,   18 U.S.C. 1791
PHILIP BERRIGAN,
ELIZABETH McALISTER,
NEIL McLAUGHLIN,
ANTHONY SCOBLICK,
JOSEPH WENDEROTH,

        Defendants.

INDICTMENT

Count I

THE GRAND JURY CHARGES:

That on or about April 1, 1970, the exact
date being to the Grand Jury unknown, and
continuously thereafter up to and including

the date of the return of this indictment, in
the Middle District of Pennsylvania and elsewhere:

EQBAL AHMAD,
PHILIP BERRIGAN
ELIZABETH McALISTER,
NEIL McLAUGHLIN,
ANTHONY SCOBLICK,
JOSEPH WENDEROTH

defendants herein, wilfully and knowingly conspired and agreed together with:

DANIEL BERRIGAN,
THOMAS DAVIDSON,
MARJORIE SHUMAN,
BEVERLY BELL,
PAUL MAYER,
WILLIAM DAVIDON,
JOGUES EGAN

Not named as defendants herein, and with
others whose names are not known to the
Grand Jury, to commit offenses against the
United States, that is, to maliciously damage
and destroy, by means of explosives, personal
and real property owned and possessed by
the United States in violation of 18 U.S.C. 844-
(f) and 18 U.S.C. 1361; to possess firearms
that is, destructive devices consisting of dynamite, "plastic explosive," primer cord and
detonating devices which had not been regis-
tered to them in the National Firearms Regis-
tration and Transfer Record as required by
Chapter 53, Title 26, U.S.C., in violation of
26 U.S.C. 5861(d); to transport explosives in
interstate commerce with knowledge and intent that they will be used to damage and
destroy real and personal property in violation
of 18 U.S.C. 844(d); and to unlawfully seize,
confine, inveigle, decoy, kidnap, abduct and
carry away and transport in interstate commerce a person for ransom, reward and otherwise in violation of 18 U.S.C. 1201.

It was part of the conspiracy that the defendants and the unindicted co-conspirators would obtain maps and diagrams of the underground tunnels in Washington, D.C., containing the heating systems for government buildings of the United States; that the defendants and unindicted co-conspirators would enter these tunnels and learn the locations of the heating pipes within the tunnels; that the defendants and unindicted co-conspirators would obtain dynamite and other explosive devices; that on George Washington's birthday in 1971 the defendants and unindicted co-conspirators would enter the underground tunnel system in Washington, D.C., and detonate explosive devices in approximately five locations in order to damage and destroy heating pipes belonging to the United States thereby rendering inoperative the heating systems in government buildings of the United States.

It was further part of the conspiracy that on the following day the defendants and unindicted co-conspirators would seize, kidnap, abduct and carry away presidential advisor Henry Kissinger, and issue a statement that his safety depends upon the satisfaction of certain demands to be made by the defendants and unindicted co-conspirators.

All of the said acts of the defendants being in violation of 18 U.S.C. 371 and 1201(c).

Overt Acts

The following overt acts were committed in furtherance of the conspiracy and to effect the object thereof:

1. On or about April 1, 1970, Philip Berrigan and Joseph Wenderoth entered underground tunnels in Washington, D.C.

2. On or about June 19, 1970, Neil McLaughlin made a telephone call to Lewisburg, Pennsylvania.

3. On or about June 22, 1970, Joseph Wenderoth and Neil McLaughlin travelled to Lewisburg, Pennsylvania.

4. On or about June 29, 1970, Philip Berrigan sent a communication from the United States Penitentiary at Lewisburg, Pennsylvania, to Elizabeth McAlister.

5. On or about July 6, 1970, Neil McLaughlin and Joseph Wenderoth travelled to Lewisburg, Pennsylvania.

6. On or about July 16, 1970, Elizabeth McAlister, Neil McLaughlin, Joseph Wenderoth, Marjorie Shuman, and Beverly Bell met in Lewisburg, Pennsylvania.

7. On or about August 10, 1970, Anthony Scoblick travelled to Lewisburg, Pennsylvania.

8. On or about August 20, 1970, Beverly Bell moved to Washington, D.C.

9. On or about August 17, 1970, Elizabeth McAlister, William Davidon, Paul Mayer, and Jogues Egan travelled to Connecticut.

10. Eqbal Ahmad, Elizabeth McAlister, Paul Mayer, Joques Egan and William Davidon met in Connecticut on or about August 17, 1970.

11. On or about August 20, 1970, Elizabeth McAlister mailed to Lewisburg, Pennsylvania, a letter for Philip Berrigan.

12. On or about August 24, 1970, Philip Berrigan sent written instructions from the United States Penitentiary at Lewisburg, Pennsylvania, to Elizabeth McAlister.

13. On or about August 19, 1970, Elizabeth McAlister made a telephone call to Lewisburg, Pennsylvania.

14. On or about August 20, 1970, Eqbal Ahmad made a telephone call to Lewisburg, Pennsylvania.

15. On or about August 22, 1970, Eqbal Ahmad made a telephone call to Lewisburg, Pennsylvania.

16. On or about August 25, 1970, Elizabeth

McAlister, Neil McLaughlin and Joseph Wenderoth met in Sea Girt, New Jersey.

17. On or about September 4, 1970, Elizabeth McAlister travelled to Danbury, Connecticut.

18. Joseph Wenderoth and Neil McLaughlin met at 43 North Water Street in Lewisburg, Pennsylvania on or about September 5, 1970.

19. On or about September 26, 1970, Elizabeth McAlister travelled to Lewisburg, Pennsylvania.

20. On or about September 20, 1970, Joseph Wenderoth discussed the Washington, D.C. tunnel system with a General Service Administration engineer.

21. On or about October 10, 1970, Joseph Wenderoth, Neil McLaughlin, Jogues Egan and Elizabeth McAlister met in Baltimore, Maryland.

22. On or about November 12, 1970, Joseph Wenderoth made a telephone call to Lewisburg, Pennsylvania.

All in violation of Title 18, United States Code, Section 371 and 1201(c).

COUNT II
THE GRAND JURY CHARGES:
That on or about the 25th day of June, 1970, in the Middle District of Pennsylvania

ELIZABETH McALISTER
contrary to rules and regulations promulgated by the Attorney General of the United States and without the knowledge and consent of the Warden of such institution, did attempt to introduce into and upon the grounds of the United States Penitentiary at Lewisburg, Pennsylvania, a package containing written communications for Philip Berrigan, in violation of 18 U.S.C. 1791.

COUNT III
THE GRAND JURY CHARGES:
That on or about the 29th day of June, 1970, in the Middle District of Pennsylvania

PHILIP BERRIGAN

contrary to rules and regulations promulgated by the Attorney General of the United States, and without the knowledge and consent of the Warden of such institution, did attempt to send from the United States Penitentiary at Lewisburg, Pennsylvania, papers containing written communications for Elizabeth McAlister in violation of 18 U.S.C. 1791.

COUNT IV

THE GRAND JURY CHARGES:

That on or about the 3rd day of August, 1970, in the Middle District of Pennsylvania

ELIZABETH McALISTER

contrary to rules and regulations promulgated by the Attorney General of the United States, and without the knowledge and consent of the Warden of such institution, did attempt to introduce into and upon the grounds of the United States Penitentiary at Lewisburg, Pennsylvania, a package containing written communications for Philip Berrigan, in violation of 18 U.S.C. 1791.

COUNT V

THE GRAND JURY CHARGES:

That on or about the 6th day of August, 1970, in the Middle District of Pennsylvania

PHILIP BERRIGAN

contrary to rules and regulations promulgated by the Attorney General of the United States and without the knowledge and consent of the Warden of such institution, did attempt to send from the United States Penitentiary at Lewisburg, Pennsylvania, papers containing written communications for Elizabeth McAlister in violation of 18 U.S.C. 1791.

COUNT VI

THE GRAND JURY CHARGES:

That on or about the 20th day of August, 1970, in the Middle District of Pennsylvania

ELIZABETH McALISTER

contrary to rules and regulations promulgated

by the Attorney General of the United States, and without the knowledge and consent of the Warden of such institution, did attempt to introduce into and upon the grounds of the United States Penitentiary at Lewisburg, Pennsylvania, a package containing written communications for Philip Berrigan, in violation of 18 U.S.C. 1791.

COUNT VII
THE GRAND JURY CHARGES:

That on or about the 24th day of August, 1970, in the Middle District of Pennsylvania

PHILIP BERRIGAN

contrary to rules and regulations promulgated by the Attorney General of the United States, and without the knowledge and consent of the Warden of such institution, did attempt to send from the United States Penitentiary at Lewisburg, Pennsylvania, papers containing written communications for Elizabeth McAlister in violation of 18 U.S.C. 1791.

A TRUE BILL

FOREMAN

S. John Cottone
United States Attorney

The Response of "The Conspiracy"

JOINT PUBLIC STATEMENT OF
DEFENDANTS AND
"CO-CONSPIRATORS,"
FEBRUARY 8, 1971

We are thirteen men and women who state with clear conscience that we are neither conspirators nor bombers nor kidnappers. In principle and in fact we have rejected all acts such as those of which we have been accused. We are a diverse group, united by a common goal: our opposition to the massive violence of our government in its war against Southeast Asia. It is because of this opposition that we have been branded a conspiracy.

Our anguish for the victims of the brutal war has led all of us to nonviolent resistance, some of us to the destruction of draft records. But, unlike our accuser, the Government of the United States, we have not advocated or engaged in violence against human beings. Unlike the Government, we have never lied to our fellow citizens about our actions. Unlike the Government, we have nothing to hide. We ask our fellow citizens to match our lives, our actions, against the actions of the President, his advisers, his chiefs of staff, and pose the question: who has committed the crimes of violence?

It is, in fact, the Government which has engaged

in kidnapping on an enormous scale: the deportation of millions of Vietnamese—and now Cambodians and Laotians—from their ancient homes by force; the adduction of American young men from their families under the Selective Service laws, sending them across state lines and international borders to be killed or maimed. It is the Government which has not only conspired but carried out the destruction by explosives of three countries: Vietnam, Laos, and Cambodia, crippling these defenseless people with napalm and pellet bombs, destroying their forests and rice fields. If one is concerned with crimes against humanity, it is the officials of the United States Government who should be on trial.

Throughout history, citizens of conscience have engaged in discussions as to how to oppose the overwhelming power of unjust governments. In such discussions, the problems of violence and nonviolence have been aired, and an infinite variety of strategies and tactics examined, accepted, or rejected. Such discussion is part of the tradition of free speech in a democratic society, protected by the First Amendment. When our Government moves against some citizens through wire-tapping, secret agents, and conspiracy laws, to turn this constitutional right into a crime, free expression is endangered for all Americans.

Our Government's disregard for the constitutional rights of individuals has marked every stage of the proceedings against us so far: the pre-indictment accusations by J. Edgar Hoover, the arrests without warrants, the excessive bail amounting to ransom, the travel restrictions on defendants and an atmosphere of intimidation created by the

Grand Jury which began historically as a shield to protect the innocent and has become instead a sword to oppress the defenseless. And most recently, we have seen a deliberate act by the Attorney General to keep the defendants from meeting together. Does justice really exist for black people, for poor people, or for those who, like us, oppose the policy of war? Based on what has happened to us so far, we can only wonder.

We believe in the holy commandment: thou shalt not kill—a commandment which our Government has violated with impunity a million times. We urge our fellow citizens to join us in demanding that our Government stop the current secret invasion of Laos, end its expansion of the war in Southeast Asia immediately and bring its troops, planes, guns, and bombs home without delay. We ask our fellow citizens to resist this war by refusing to fight, refusing to pay taxes, refusing to cooperate in any way. Finally, we reaffirm our dedication to a world without violence—that violence which for so long has ravaged so many lands, so many souls.

Dr. Eqbal Ahmad
Sr. Beverly Bell
Fr. Daniel Berrigan
Fr. Philip Berrigan
William Davidon
Tom Davidson

Sr. Jogues Egan
Fr. Paul Mayer
Sr. Elizabeth McAlister
Fr. Neil McLaughlin
Anthony Scoblick
Marjorie Shuman

Fr. Joseph Wenderoth

Contributors

William Van Etten Casey was born in Boston in 1914. He entered the Jesuit order in 1932 and was ordained a priest in 1944. He took his B.A. and M.A. in English at Boston College and holds licentiates in Philosophy and in Theology from Weston College, Weston, Massachusetts. He has taught at Boston College, where he was also Chairman of the Department of Theology and, later, Dean and Academic Vice President. Since 1960 he has been Professor of Theology at Holy Cross College. He has edited *Holy Cross Quarterly* since 1969. In 1962–63 Fr. Casey was in residence at the American School of Oriental Research in Jerusalem and was on the staff of an archaeological expedition in Jordan. In 1967–68 he was Director of the American School of Oriental Research in Jerusalem. Fr. Casey has lectured widely on biblical archaeology, the Middle East, the Book of Job, and other subjects, and has contributed to *America, Commonweal, Extension, The New York Times,* and other publications.

Philip Nobile is a 1964 graduate of Holy Cross. His reportage has appeared in *The New York*

Review of Books and *The New York Times Magazine.* He is the editor of several recent and forthcoming books including THE NEW EROTICISM, THE GREENING OF AMERICA CONTROVERSY, and THE COMPLETE ECOLOGY FACTBOOK (with John Deedy). A former editor of *Commonweal,* Mr. Nobile is a regular political reporter for *The National Catholic Reporter.* His article "Phil Berrigan in Prison" first appeared in *The New York Review of Books;* it was reprinted in the special Berrigan issue of *Holy Cross Quarterly* and has been expanded considerably for its inclusion in this book.

Edward Duff, S.J., is a graduate of Holy Cross and is Associate Professor of Political Science there. He holds a doctorate in political science from the Graduate School of International Studies of the University of Geneva, Switzerland. Fr. Duff has contributed to many periodicals and is the author of THE SOCIAL THOUGHT OF THE WORLD COUNCIL OF CHURCHES. His article "The Burden of the Berrigans" was written for the special issue of *Holy Cross Quarterly* and was reprinted in slightly revised form in *The New Republic.* It is this revised version that is included in this book.

Richard J. Clifford, S.J., was a student at Holy Cross in 1952–53 and an instructor in classics there from 1960 to 1962. He received his doctorate in Old Testament from Harvard in 1970 and currently teaches at Weston School of Theology in Cambridge, Massachusetts. His article "The Berrigans: Prophetic?" was written for the *Quarterly*.

Noam Chomsky is the distinguished scholar and influential thinker in the field of linguistics. His most recent book is AT WAR WITH ASIA. His article "On the Limits of Civil Disobedience" was written for the *Quarterly*.

Robert McAfee Brown is a Presbyterian minister, Professor of Religion at Stanford University, and noted author. His article "The Berrigans: Signs or Models?" was written for the *Quarterly*; it has been revised slightly for inclusion in this book.

David J. O'Brien is Associate Professor of History at Holy Cross. He holds a B.A. from Notre Dame and a Ph.D. from the University of Rochester. He has contributed to periodicals and is the author of AMERICAN CATHOLICS AND SOCIAL REFORM: THE NEW DEAL YEARS. His article "The Berrigans and America" was written for the *Quarterly* and has been revised slightly for inclusion in this book.

John C. Raines is Assistant Professor of Religion at Temple University. He is a graduate of Carleton College and Union Theological Seminary. Dr. Raines co-edited MARXISM AND RADICAL RELIGION. He is the minister who introduced Fr. Daniel Berrigan to the congregation of the First United Methodist Church of Germantown, Pa., when Fr. Berrigan surfaced to preach there during the four months of his flight from federal agents. His article "The Followers of Life" was written for the *Quarterly*.

Gordon C. Zahn is the distinguished author of WAR, CONSCIENCE AND DISSENT, GERMAN CATHOLICS AND HITLER'S WARS, WHAT IS SOCIETY? and many other books and articles. His essay "The Berrigans: Radical Activism Personified" first appeared in *Catholic World*.

Rosemary Radford Ruether teaches religion at Howard University in Washington, D.C. She is the author of THE CHURCH WITHIN and THE RADICAL KINGDOM. Her article "Beyond Confrontation: The Therapeutic Task" was written especially for this book.

Francine du Plessix Gray writes for *The New Yorker* and is the author of DIVINE DISOBEDIENCE: PROFILES IN CATHOLIC RADICALISM. She spent part of 1970 in Hawaii, where her husband, the painter Cleve Gray, was artist-in-residence at the Academy of Fine Arts in Honolulu, and where the conversation "Phil Berrigan in Hawaii" was taped. It first appeared in the *Quarterly*.

Jim Forest, a former editor of *The Catholic Worker* and *Liberation*, is a co-chairman of the Catholic Peace Fellowship. He served a year in federal prison for his part in the "Milwaukee Fourteen" draft board action. Currently, he is living in a work collective in Emmaus House in East Harlem, New York City. His article "Philip Berrigan: Disturber of Sleep" was written especially for this book.

Paul Cowan is the author of THE MAKING OF AN UN-AMERICAN. He contributes regularly to *Commentary, Ramparts,* and *The Voice.* His article "Father Dan Berrigan: Fugitive from Injustice" first appeared in *The Voice.* Mr. Cowan is also responsible, with two others, for preparing Fr. Daniel Berrigan's "Letter to the Weathermen" for publication. Fr. Berrigan had spoken from rough notes, and repetitions and outdated references were excised when the tape surfaced several months later. Fr. Berrigan then approved the suggested cuts and condensations. The letter also appeared in *The Voice.*

Robert Coles is at work on a continuing study of men, women, and children involved in social struggles in different parts of the United States which will be published in three volumes called CHILDREN OF CRISIS. The first volume, A STUDY OF COURAGE AND FEAR, appeared in 1967. MIGRANTS, SHARECROPPERS AND MOUNTAINEERS and THE SOUTH GOES NORTH will be published at the end of 1971 and the beginning of 1972. A book of his dialogues with Fr. Daniel Berrigan, THE GEOGRAPHY OF FAITH, will be published in the fall of 1971. His article "Thinking About Those Priests" was written especially for this book.

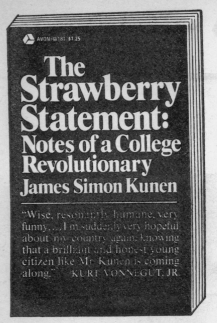